THE END OF LIFE AS WE KNOW IT

STARVING

CAN WE FEED EVERYONE?

LISA A. WROBLE

Enslow Publishing
101 W. 23rd Street
Suite 240
New York, NY 10011
USA
enslow.com

Published in 2016 by Enslow Publishing, LLC
101 W. 23rd Street, Suite 240, New York, NY 10011

Library of Congress Cataloging-in-Publication Data

Wroble, Lisa A., author.
Starving : can we feed everyone? / Lisa A. Wroble.
pages cm. — (The end of life as we know it)
Includes bibliographical references and index.
Summary: "Describes the problems facing our planet concerning food"— Provided by publisher.
ISBN 978-0-7660-7374-6
1. Food security—Juvenile literature. 2. Food supply—Juvenile literature. 3. Sustainable agriculture—Juvenile literature. 4. Starvation—Prevention—Juvenile literature. I. Title.
HD9000.5.W76 2016
363.8–dc23
2015030363

Printed in the United States of America

To Our Readers: We have done our best to make sure all website addresses in this book were active and appropriate when we went to press. However, the author and the publisher have no control over and assume no liability for the material available on those websites or on any websites they may link to. Any comments or suggestions can be sent by e-mail to customerservice@enslow.com.

Portions of this book originally appeared in the book *Food for a Greener Planet: What You Can Do.*

Photo Credits: Cover, Gajus/Shutterstock.com; p. 4 Frank Whitney/Photographer's Choice/Getty Images; p. 7 Brent Winebrenner/ Lonely Planet Images/Getty Images; p. 8 Pavel L Photo and Video/ Shutterstock.com; p. 10 Monkey Business Images/Shutterstock.com; p. 14 Sean Gallup/Getty Images News/Getty Images; p. 18 Sean Pavone/Shutterstock.com; p. 20 Jonathan Feinstein/Shutterstock.com; p. 24 David Joel/The Images Bank/Getty Images; p. 26 Brent Hofacker/Shutterstpock.com; p. 29 Jeeranan Thongpan/Shutterstock.com; p. 32 Robert George Young/Photographer's Choice/Getty Images; p. 34 Dar1930/Shutterstock.com; p. 38 Joel Sartore/National Geographic/Getty Images; p. 40 Tony Page/The Images Bank/Getty Images; p. 42 Pete McBride/National Geographic/Getty Images; p. 44 David Reede/All Canada Photos/Getty Images; p. 47 Chris R. Sharp/Science Source/Getty Images; p. 50 Gaiger/Topical Press Agency/Hulton Archive/Getty Images; pp. 53, 74 © AP Images; p. 55 Terrence Spencer/The LIFE Images Collection/Getty Images; p. 57 Art Rickerby/The LIFE Picture Collection/Getty Images; p. 60 Alfred Eisenstaedt/The LIFE Picture Collection/Getty Images; p. 64 mexrix/Shutterstock.com; p. 66 Neil Bradfield/Shutterstock.com; p. 69 wawritto/Shutterstock.com; p. 72 MartinMaritz/Shutterstock.com; p. 78 © iStockphoto.com/pjohnson1; p. 80 Leonid Ikan/Shutterstock.com; p. 83 clearviewstock/Shutterstock.com; p 86 ALEXANDER JOE/AFP/Getty Images; p. 89 Martin Fowler/Shutterstock.com; p. 92 Noah Berger/Bloomberg via Getty Images; p. 96 Christian Mueller/Shutterstock.com; p. 99 Patrick Smith/Getty Images News/Getty Images; p. 101 © Citizen of the Planet/Alamy; p. 103 © Ros Drinkwater/Alamy.

CONTENTS

In America, food is all around us. Despite its abundance, however, we are in the midst of a serious crisis when it comes to the production and consumption of food.

INTRODUCTION

HIGH ALERT! FOOD CRISIS

FOOD IN AMERICA IS A BIG DEAL. IT'S ALL AROUND us—in TV ads, on billboards, and in the hundreds of choices we have daily for eating. Food is at our fingertips—and not just from the grocery store. Vending machines, cafeterias, delis, cafés, fast food restaurants, food courts, food trucks, and food stands on the street are just some of the many choices. It's easy to eat on the run. Most Americans do.

Each year the average American consumes 1,966 pounds of food, according to the US Department of Agriculture (USDA).[1] That's nearly one ton of food—the weight of a small car. Teens alone spend 18 percent of their own money on food. That's $16.4 billion per year, according to a report by FONA International, a company that produces flavors used in food and beverage production. Many teens also have input regarding how the family food budget is spent, including 88 percent on snacks, 87 percent on cereal, and 83 percent on beverages.[2]

So how can our nation be in a food crisis?

Most Americans have no idea how our food is grown, let alone how our bodies use it. We eat for convenience. It's beginning to adversely affect our health. Most Americans have no idea that, according to the Food and Agriculture Organization (FAO) of the United Nations, each year one-third of the total food grown worldwide is lost or wasted "along the chain that stretches from farm to processing plants, market places, retailers, food-service operations, and our collective kitchens." This amounts to 2.8 trillion pounds of food.[3] Meanwhile, nearly fifty million people in the United States are starving.[4]

"The state of food in America is not a happy story," says Carol Boutard of Ayers Creek Farm in Oregon. "The industrial [farming] model is not interested in flavor or in quality."[5] The food chain is seriously broken.

Access to fresh fruits and vegetables is limited. This is especially true in big cities. The average teen eats only one to two servings of vegetables and fruit per day, according to an analysis by the Centers for Disease Control and Prevention (CDC). The suggested daily serving is four to five.[6] But when teens grow food in school gardens, their attitudes change.

"I love my vegetables," says Michelle Simpson, a senior at Heritage High School in Baltimore, Maryland. She proudly shows visitors to Hoop Village the kale and cabbage she helped plant. Hoop Village is an urban farming program that uses three plastic-covered greenhouses to teach skills in agriculture, horticulture, and marketing. In addition to providing jobs, students market their produce to the northeast Baltimore community.[7]

This is one of many such programs in the nation. Throughout the United States, students are learning about growing food. These programs are increasing. More than one in four schools, mostly elementary, now have learning gardens.[8] Many programs sell the harvest to local markets,

Today, many schools have programs that teach children how to plant and harvest their own fruits and vegetables.

restaurants, and their own school cafeterias. So students have access to fresh produce, at least in school.

When produce is available at the store, the cost keeps many families from buying it. According to food writer Marion Nestle, the relative cost of fresh fruits and vegetables has risen 40 percent since 1980, while the relative cost of processed food has gone down by about 40 percent. This encourages Americans to spend their food budgets on "the cheapest calories you can get, and that is going to be processed food. And that has to do with our farm policy."[9]

The more we choose packaged and highly processed foods, the greater the impact on our health. The CDC states that more than one-third of children and teens are overweight or obese. The number of obese teens ages twelve to nineteen quadrupled over a thirty-year period. It rose from 5 percent in 1980 and remains steady at 21 percent today.[10]

This is happening across the globe. For the first time, obesity is on the rise in developing countries, such as Africa. It exists alongside malnutrition. This is because both are symptoms of the same thing: poor nutrition. The body does not get the nutrients it needs. In obesity, the body gets plenty of food—sometimes too much. But that food does not have all the body needs to be healthy.

It's not only the cost to our health that is causing a food crisis. Current farming methods have an impact on the planet. It's estimated that one-fifth of fossil fuel use goes toward growing, packaging, and transporting food.[11]

Farms raising meat and poultry also add to the problem. The animal waste creates noxious fumes that add to greenhouse gases. Chemicals

Modern farming methods are taking their toll on the food supply, as well as adding to the problem of global warming. Huge farms that produce one crop or raise one kind of animal are harmful to the environment.

used for crops hinder air quality and also enter water supplies. Big business farming plays a role in global warming, which can cause fewer crops at harvest.

The current farming model is not working. The companies growing and raising our food say it is the only way to have enough food for everyone. Yet we have both starvation and obesity at alarming rates. Both are signs of poor nutrition.

Can we possibly feed everyone and save the planet, too? Yes, says Dr. Phillipe Desborses, an environmental scientist. We can grow healthy food and enough food in a sustainable way. First, "we have to stop poisoning the earth, the air, and our food with the false excuse that we're feeding mankind when in fact we're starving mankind," Desborses said at an FAO United Nations conference in Europe.[12]

In India and Africa, they have started using agroecology to grow food. This is another term for sustainable farming. Sustainable agriculture is a type of farming. It ensures the land used to grow food will be healthy and able to grow different foods for many, many generations. Sustainable farming asks that we become stewards of the land. This means we take care not to pollute soil, air, or water. It asks that we understand how soil, air, water, and sunlight work together to grow food and raise livestock. The result is quality food and bigger harvests. This means better nutrition and enough food for all.

We need to act now. This begins with awareness. It begins with understanding how our bodies use food, how our food is grown, how it's packaged, and how to be stewards of the planet.

The cost of this food crisis is too high to ignore.

We often take food for granted, and don't take the time to think about what or how much we are eating.

CHAPTER 1

FUEL UP WITH FOOD

IN NORTH AMERICA, WE ARE FORTUNATE TO BE SURROUNDED by food. We have many options for a fast and easy meal. We don't stop at three meals a day. Snacks are frequent. Grab a candy bar or cookies. Vending machines willingly dump out sodas and chips at the drop of several quarters. Want something more filling? How about ice cream, a soft pretzel, or a hot dog? Hang out with friends for a slice of pizza or a muffin and a latte at the local coffee shop. If you need to head to practice or work, protein bars and energy drinks help you hold out until dinnertime. We are overwhelmed with food, and our waistlines show it.

ENCOURAGED TO EAT MORE

Our food choices are influenced by advertising. Children watch more than ten food-related ads every day, states a report by the Prevention Institute.[1] That's four thousand per year. Ninety-eight percent of the food ads feature products high in fat, sugar, or salt and low in fiber. These ads have an impact. We are a population that enjoys fast, quick meals that are sweet, starchy, and flavorful. Even meals made at home tend to be from boxes. We open a package, heat, and eat. Or, we combine several canned or boxed foods to make casseroles or some other meal. Ads and magazines tell us how fast and easy it is to make a home-cooked meal. The portions are big to fill us up. In fact, take a close look at single-serve packages of chips, nuts, or some other snack. Chances are that the package is meant as more than one serving. We are encouraged to overeat. Still, we opt for nighttime snacks in front of the computer or TV before bed.

CHILDHOOD HUNGER

Despite plenty of food, 795 million people in the world do not have enough food to lead a healthy, active life. That's one in nine people on the planet, according to a World Food Programme (WFP) report.[2] In the United States, 49.1 million people are food insecure. This means they do not know where their next meal is coming from, and they often go hungry. It impacts every county in every state in the country. Of these food insecure people, 15.8 million are children and teens.[3] In Canada, the count is one million children, or one in six.[4] While many of these children are helped with free school breakfasts and lunches, they face hunger at other times. In the evenings and on weekends, they have no access to school-provided food.

Despite the abundance of food most North Americans enjoy, we are experiencing a food crisis. Instead of being healthy, many of us are overweight. In the United States, 21 percent of young people aged twelve to nineteen are considered overweight.[5] According to the Childhood Obesity Foundation, obesity rates in Canada have risen steadily in recent decades. Twenty-nine percent of Canadian youth aged two to seventeen are considered overweight or obese.[6] This means the amount of body fat in relation to height and weight is outside the normal ranking of 5th to 85th percentile. A percentile between 85 and 95 is considered overweight, while a percentile above 95 is considered obese.[7] It comes down to food choices. Fast and prepackaged foods are convenient, but they pile on the calories. They may help us feel full, but they lack key nutrients. It is the type of food we consume that creates the problem.

OUR BODIES USE FOOD AS FUEL

The food we eat is a mix of thousands of compounds. Our bodies use the nutrients in whatever we eat. The body breaks down the food to get at those nutrients. This is called digestion. It begins in the mouth where saliva breaks down carbohydrates, such as grains and starches. It continues in the stomach and small intestines. Gastric juices break down what we have eaten. Carbohydrates become simple sugars. Proteins are broken down into amino acids. Fats are broken down into fatty acids. The body absorbs the nutrients through the walls of the intestines. Whatever is left leaves the body as waste.

Nutrients are grouped into six categories. We need some of these nutrients in large amounts. These are called macronutrients. Carbohydrates, protein, water, and fat are the nutrients we need most. We need two types of nutrients in smaller amounts. These are called micronutrients. They are the vitamins and minerals found in the foods we eat.

The body needs nutrients for three functions. Nutrients provide energy, growth, and continued health. Nutrients in food provide fuel for energy. The body first burns the sugars from carbohydrates. This allows energy for moving, thinking, and even breathing. In addition, it gives the body energy to use the other nutrients. Amino acids and fatty acids are used to build or repair body cells and tissues. They also help maintain body systems and keep the whole body running smoothly. If the body needs to, it can also burn fatty acids for energy. Extra nutrients, such as fats or proteins, are stored by the body to use later. The body stores them as fat. So, if we eat more than we need to, those extra calories are also stored as fat.[8]

When people do not get enough to eat, they become undernourished. This means their bodies are starved for nutrients. They are not getting the protein, fats, carbohydrates, vitamins, or minerals needed to be healthy. Severe undernourishment is called malnutrition. Food programs in poor countries, such as those in Africa, try to prevent the hunger that can lead to malnutrition. Even people who are not starving in these countries may not get enough nutrition. Lack of needed nutrients can cause illness. When the body is weakened, it cannot protect itself from disease.

Fresh vegetables provide our bodies with essential nutrients that we don't get from food that comes in a box.

TAKE ACTION!

TRACK TYPES OF FOOD YOU EAT

The next time you eat a snack, check the wrapper. How many of the ingredients are hard to pronounce? These foods, which we open and eat, are prepackaged. They are highly processed. Refined flour, sugar, flavorings, and preservatives add up to yummy tastes. But how much of it is your body able to use?

Try this. Track the different types of food you eat for a week. Mark whether the food is prepackaged, frozen (heat and eat), instant (add water or milk and eat), or fresh vegetables, fruits, or nuts.

Fresh food is whole food. It is not made in a factory. It is not processed into food products. It does not have refined sugar or flour added.

After a week, look at your results. Do you need more fresh food and less food full of refined flour, sugar, fat, and preservatives?

When fresh food is not available, dried fruits are good snacking choices. They are processed, but not like cakes, cookies, chips, candy, and snack foods. The processing dries the fruit. Sometimes a preservative is added. But you will be able to read and pronounce the ingredients on these packages. According to food writer Cheryl Redmond, "Whole fruits and vegetables offer vitamins in a form your body uses best." She explains that even vitamin makers have not been able to copy "the way nature's bounty preserves and delivers these nutrients."[9]

This balance of eating and getting the right nutrients is important for every living thing. If a plant does not get what it needs from the soil, it will grow, but it may not be healthy. The animals we eat for meat also eat plants for food. If the plants are not healthy, animals will not be healthy.

If both the plants and meat we eat do not get the nutrients they need, our bodies will not get the nutrients we need.

LACKING NUTRIENTS

All living things need food. Green plants use sunlight to make food. The sun gives plants energy. This energy helps plants turn water, minerals from the soil, and carbon dioxide, a gas from the air, into food. The food allows plants to grow. People and animals use the food made by plants for energy. People get food from plants, but most people also get food by eating animals. Those animals eat plants for food. If the animals eat poor quality food, they will not provide the best nutrients for us.

Basic foods we get from plants are grains, vegetables, fruits, and nuts. Animals provide meat, eggs, and milk. For variety, people combine these basic foods to create other foods. Milk is turned into cheese or yogurt. Grains are made into bread or cereal. The most common grains in North America are corn, wheat, and rice.

In developing countries, such as those in Africa, the main foods come from plants, including grain. In developed countries, such as the United States, meat or food from animals makes up a greater part of the diet. Though many foods, such as eggs, fruits, and vegetables, are sold in their whole, natural form, animals are butchered into cuts of meat for the market. The meat is then cooked. Herbs, mushrooms, and spices are added to meat and other cooked dishes. They add flavor and variety.

When fruits and vegetables are picked and eaten, they are called fresh, whole foods. When vegetables, herbs, and meats are cooked together, they are called simple food. Both types of food are close to the way nature gave them to us. They are filled with nutrients. Once food is picked, though, it

OBESITY ON THE RISE

Even when people have more than enough to eat, they can become unhealthy. Many Americans have plenty of food but poor health. They eat the wrong kinds of foods. Or the food they eat does not include enough nutrients. Nutrients are needed to maintain body systems. They keep the whole body healthy. Both undernourishment and malnutrition can happen even when people have plenty to eat. According to the Food and Agriculture Organization of the United Nations, both undernutrition and obesity are now problems in developing countries.[10]

Obesity can happen when we eat foods with too many of the wrong nutrients, such as carbohydrates and fats. The body does not need many of them, so they are often stored. Meanwhile, the body suffers because it still needs vitamins, minerals, or protein. The body sends signals that nutrients are needed, so people keep eating. Unless they eat the right foods, their bodies will still need certain vitamins and minerals. The body starves for what it needs, yet plenty of food is available.

Jim Goodman, an organic farmer in Wisconsin and policy board member of the Organic Consumers Association, blames the way food is grown. "According to the USDA," he says, "Americans are increasingly deficient in calcium, potassium, magnesium, and vitamins A, C, D, and E." He explains that the lower levels of vitamins, minerals, and other nutrients in the foods we eat mean the soil on farms is depleted. This means the soil is worn out. If the soil does not have enough of the right nutrients for the plants to be healthy, the food from the plants will not have enough of the nutrients our bodies need. Goodman says this poor soil quality is "caused by industrial farming practices."[11]

The availability of fast food is contributing to the problem of obesity in America.

loses tiny amounts of nutrients. So, as it sits waiting to be eaten, more and more nutrients leach away. Meat must be kept cold after it is butchered. It must also be cooked soon after, or it will spoil.

The more that is done to food to make it ready for us to eat, the less nutritious it becomes. This is why it is important to understand where food comes from—to know how food is grown, picked, and shipped. It is also important to know how some food is packaged and processed before it reaches the market.

THE PROBLEM WITH PACKAGED FOODS

Much of the food from farms goes to food-packing plants. Some is packaged whole to ship to stores and markets. Most is turned into ready-to-eat or quick-to-make foods. The steps taken to do this are called food processing. This change from fresh food to ready-to-eat food products changes the quality of the food we eat most often during the day.

Look down the aisles at any supermarket. They are filled with canned, dried, and frozen foods. These foods are all prepared at food packing plants. Some foods are processed. This means they are combined to make new foods like canned soup, pasta sauce, and baked goods, such as bread, cakes, and muffins. Refined sugar, flour, salt, and preservatives are often added during processing. The preservatives allow these foods to last longer on the shelf without spoiling. Food packing plants also make frozen dinners, microwave meals, and mix-and-eat instant food products. These are all called convenience foods. They make it easy to fix a meal or a snack. If they are not ready to open and eat, they are fast to make and eat.

These foods might taste yummy to some individuals, especially when compared to snacking on vegetables. But remember that the body needs certain nutrients to be healthy. Our bodies use the nutrients in the food we eat. Whole, fresh foods are loaded with nutrients our bodies can use. They do not contain additives our bodies do not need. This is why whole, fresh food is the best food choice. Healthy food fortifies the body. "Plant cells offer the perfect protective environment for vitamins, minerals, and phytochemicals like flavonoids," explains food writer Cheryl Redmond. Plant cells keep these nutrients protected. They will stay powerful and give the body plenty to use to stay healthy.[12] Eating fresh, whole food helps fight disease. It may even slow down aging because antioxidants in plant foods keep our skin cells healthy.

Supermarkets tend to place prepackaged food in the center aisles and produce, dairy, and meat along the perimeter of the store.

CHAPTER 2

PACKAGED FOR EASE AND APPEAL

MOST OF US GET OUR FOOD FROM A GROCERY STORE or market. Many larger stores are set up with the prepackaged and frozen items in the middle aisles. Select from row after row of cereals, cookies, crackers, canned, and frozen foods. Along the perimeter are whole, fresh foods. Fresh foods are often the ingredients used to make meals. They are closest to their natural state. For example, along the outer edges of the store, you'll find dairy products and eggs, fresh meat and seafood counters, the bakery, and fresh fruits and vegetables. You may have noticed signs near fruits or vegetables in the store or labels on the foods themselves that say "Product of Mexico" or "Grown in Brazil." That is a long way to travel. And, based on the number of inner aisles at the grocery store, our food is transformed once it is picked. Much of it travels a long way to reach us.

All food is grown or raised. Vegetables and grains, such as oats and wheat, are grown on farms. Fruits and most nuts are grown in orchards or groves. These are farms with acres of trees of the same type—an orchard of apple trees, for instance, or a citrus grove with sections of orange, lemon, lime, and grapefruit trees.

Meat is raised on farms, too. Sometimes these farms are called ranches. Beef comes from cattle raised on cattle ranches. Pork comes from hogs. When the animals are grown, they are sent to a slaughterhouse. There the meat is cut and sent to markets and butcher shops.

LOST AND WASTED FOOD

The Food and Agriculture Organization of the United Nations monitors what is grown and eaten around the world. They report that one-third, some 2.8 trillion pounds, of all food grown globally is lost or wasted each year. Food loss means that some of the crop was damaged during harvest or in preparing it for shipping. Or the food was rejected by the buyers for restaurants or food packaging plants. Sometimes it is food left in the field because it does not get picked quickly enough. It often gets plowed under. Food waste is food thrown away by consumers or retailers. This might be food that reaches the expiration date, is uneaten or not sold by restaurants, or improperly stored.[1] These are examples of a severe breakdown in the food chain. The waste not only impacts the hungry, but it also adds to the costs of energy and labor used to grow food. Additionally, decomposing produce creates methane, a greenhouse gas, which environmental writer Elizabeth Royte explains.[2] Given this waste, we *are* growing enough food to feed everyone in the world. The problem exists in how to get it into everyone's mouths.

A poultry farm raises hens for eggs and meat. A dairy farm raises cows for milk. The milk is sold to a dairy plant, which bottles the milk and makes cheese and yogurt.

When the food is ripe it is picked. This is called harvesting. This fresh food is called raw or whole food. Some raw food is shipped to stores.

MAKING FOOD CONVENIENT

Most whole, fresh food is sold to food plants, or companies that make the food ready to eat. Eggs are packed in cartons. Milk is made into cheese. Beef and pork are made into lunch meat. Grain is ground into flour. Even sugar needs to be made. It is refined from sugar beets or sugarcane to make white sugar. These foods are all made or prepared in food plants. Then they are packaged and shipped to stores.

Some of these foods are used to make other food. Snack cakes and muffins use eggs, flour, and refined sugar. These are called processed foods. We open the package and eat them. For example, breakfast bars, cookies, muffins, and snack cakes are ready to eat out of the package. To eat other foods, a little preparation is needed. For example, we might open a loaf of bread and lunch meat to make a sandwich or open a box of cereal and a bottle of milk to make a quick breakfast. Some processed foods need to be heated and then served. Frozen dinners, a can of soup, or hot dogs are examples.

Packaged foods are also called convenience foods. Without them we would have a lot of work to do before we could eat. For example, to make a peanut butter and jelly sandwich, you would have to bake bread, grind peanuts into peanut butter, and wash, peel, mash, and cook fruit into jelly. Of course, you would have enough for many sandwiches. But when all of these foods are made for us, they make life easier.

A factory in Louisville, Kentucky, where biscuits are made. Packaged food such as this is convenient but not always the healthiest choice.

PROCESSING MEAT

Processing makes meat safer to eat. Animals raised for meat are sent to a butcher shop or slaughterhouse. A butcher usually handles only a few animals at a time. A slaughterhouse handles many. According to investigative writer Eric Schlosser, "Twenty years ago, new meatpacking plants in the High Plains slaughtered about 175 cattle an hour." Today, faster equipment allows them to slaughter 400 cattle an hour.[3] Meatpacking plants are large slaughterhouses often owned by companies that raise the animals. For example, Smithfield Foods, one of the largest pork producers, owns 1.2 million sows, which give birth to the pigs raised for food. The company also slaughters the pigs and packages pork products sold in grocery stores.[4]

Whether the company is large or small, the animal is first killed. Then the carcass is prepared. The parts of the animal that we do not eat, such as the gut, organs, skin, head, and legs, are removed. If this is not done properly, the meat will spoil. For example, animal feces from the gut could pollute the meat.[5]

Then the carcass is divided into sections. These sections are trimmed into different cuts of meat. Like produce from a farm, some meat is sent to food packing plants, where it is processed into ready-to-eat food. Some meat is sent to stores. The butcher at the store cuts the meat into smaller portions. Some is ground to make hamburgers or sausage. Without people to cut meat and make it ready to eat, we would have to do this work before we could cook the meat.

IMPROVING FLAVOR AND TEXTURE

When fresh foods are blended to make new foods, such as sausage, bread, or muffins, salt and spices are added. These improve the flavor. Food packing plants also add other ingredients. They are called food additives. These make the food look and taste better. Some are added to help hold the food together—so muffins are not too crumbly or so oil in peanut butter does not separate as it sits on a shelf.

The Food and Drug Administration (FDA) regulates food additives. According to the FDA website, "Additives have been used for many years to preserve, flavor, blend, thicken and color foods."[6] Additives allow food

Many breakfast cereals are full of preservatives, as well as artificial colors and flavors.

to be stored long past harvest. They keep the food fresh and make it more appealing. Cooking food sometimes makes it lose color. Food dyes are added to change the coloring so we will want to eat it.

Color is not the only thing lost when food is cooked. Cooking food changes the texture, and nutrients are sometimes lost. According to the *USDA Table of Nutrient Retention Factors,* the amount of nutrients lost depends on how the food is cooked. Higher temperatures often leach more nutrients, yet freezing retains up to 95 percent of the nutrients.[7] Boiling vegetables, for example, releases water-soluble vitamins, which are then lost when the water is drained before serving. Additives are used to replace lost nutrients during food processing. This is called enriching the food product. Sometimes additives are used to boost the nutrients

CHEMICALS IN FOOD

When we read ingredients lists on foods, some words are hard to pronounce. They sound like chemicals from a laboratory. Many people assume that food additives are chemicals. Chemicals in food must be harmful. In truth, all foods are made up of chemicals. An orange plucked from a tree contains ascorbic acid, which is also called vitamin C. Ascorbic acid may be added to foods to boost nutrition or to delay spoiling. This additive may come from oranges or it may be made in a laboratory. Both are identical.

Like that orange, food that is grown and animals that are raised for meat contain chemicals. The FDA says that every living thing is made of "the chemical building blocks of carbon, hydrogen, nitrogen, oxygen, and other elements."[8] These combine to make proteins, fats, starches, water, and vitamins, which are in our bodies—and in foods we eat.

in foods to make them healthier. This is called fortifying the product. Energy bars and cereal are two examples of fortified foods.

Concern over chemicals in foods is linked with preservatives, or chemicals added to keep food from spoiling. Preservatives are important. Much of the shelf-stable food we buy does not need to be stored in the refrigerator. Once the food is opened, it will spoil. This is when we need to store it in the refrigerator. These packaged foods use preservatives so they can stay on store shelves longer.

There are two types of preservatives added to food. One type is antimicrobial. These preservatives keep mold, yeast, and bacteria from growing. The other type is antioxidant. These curb the reaction between air, light, and heat with the food. They keep the food from turning brown or rancid. They also protect essential amino acids in food. Amino acids are the building blocks of proteins.[9]

Foods that come ready to open, heat, and eat, such as TV dinners or frozen pizzas, go through more preparation. Many ingredients are processed and then combined to create the meal. For example, for the frozen pizza, dough and sauce are made, then the cheese, meat, and vegetable toppings are prepared. These meals are known as heavily processed foods. They often contain more preservatives than foods used to cook a meal at home.

WAYS TO KEEP FOOD FRESH

Adding chemicals to food is not the only way to keep it fresh. Different methods are also used. Many have been used for centuries. Salting meat was used by ancient Egyptians.[10] Ancient Egyptians also dried fruit, beans, and fish to store for later use.[11] Some foods we enjoy today were early ways to store food. Pickling is an example of this. Vegetables, meat, or fish are soaked in saltwater brine for many days. Then they are drained and stored in vinegar. The most popular item is pickled cucumbers, or pickles. Cheese is another example. Enzymes added to milk change the taste and texture. And cheese lasts much longer than the milk it is made from.

All food contains natural enzymes. These are proteins that ripen or age food. Once food is picked, the enzymes break down, and the food begins to spoil. When food is left on the kitchen counter, bacteria and microorganisms also cause spoilage.[12] Washing the skins of vegetables and fruits removes some bacteria. Placing food in the refrigerator slows the bacteria and enzymes down. Food does not spoil as quickly. Freezing

Fresh food, such as these strawberries, will go bad after a certain length of time. Techniques such as canning and freezing can increase the life of some foods.

stops the process. The enzymes and bacteria become inactive. When the food is thawed and opened, the process begins again.

Another way to stop bacteria is to sterilize food. Boiling or heating food to high temperatures kills bacteria. Canning uses this process. Food is placed in jars or cans, which are sealed with lids and then heated. As the food inside is sterilized, the container seals. The bacteria are killed. The seal keeps new bacteria out. Canned food can be stored on the shelf for a long time. Once it is opened, though, bacteria can get in. This is why opened cans and jars are stored in the refrigerator.

Cans and jars are not the only containers used for canning today. Foil pouches of tuna, plastic cups of fruit, and boxes of juice are all canned. Juice and milk found in boxes on grocery store shelves use a special canning method. Ultra high temperature (UHT) pasteurization kills bacteria using a high temperature for two seconds.[13] Because the beverage is sterilized and sealed, it does not need to be refrigerated.

Most milk is pasteurized. All milk contains natural bacteria. Left at room temperature, it spoils within several hours. Refrigerating helps. But it still spoils in a day. Boiling milk to sterilize it changes the taste. Pasteurization does not change the taste. The milk is heated to a temperature high enough to kill some of the bacteria and stop the enzymes. This milk can be stored in the refrigerator for about a week.

Drying food also prevents spoilage. In dried, or dehydrated, food the water is removed. It can be stored in airtight containers for a very long time. The texture and taste of the food is changed, and new foods are the result. Raisins are dried grapes. Prunes are dried plums. Drying brings out the natural sugar in fruits, so they taste sweeter than fresh fruit.

Freeze-drying is another way to dehydrate food. The taste does not change as much as in drying. In freeze-drying, food is frozen then placed in a strong vacuum. Water in the food freezes. The vacuum causes it to change from ice into vapor. The water, or liquid, stage is skipped. Instant coffee is made through freeze-drying.

A less common method is irradiation, which uses nuclear radiation to kill almost all the bacteria. It does not sterilize the food, though. Food can be sealed in plastic and irradiated. Since it is sealed, new bacteria cannot get in, so the package is safe to store on a shelf. This method does not change the flavor or texture of food. Thirty-seven

TAKE ACTION!

READ FOOD LABELS

What nutrition are you really getting from the foods you eat? Food labels can help you figure it out. Our bodies use only the nutrients in our food. They get rid of the rest. Foods with a lot of preservatives, food dyes, and artificial ingredients don't add to our nutrition. The ingredients are listed under the nutrition facts box. Ingredients are listed in quantity order by weight. For example, flour is listed first in bread, cakes, and muffins. Additives are included at the end because they are used in small amounts. Be sure to look at the front of the box, too. If you see "enriched" or "fortified," it means the product is heavily processed. Nutrients lost during processing are added back. Often these vitamins and minerals are harder for our bodies to use than the nutrients in the food's natural or whole form.

Pay attention to the nutritional information and ingredients lists on packaged food. The ingredients are listed from greatest amount to least amount.

countries, including the United States, have deemed irradiation safe for forty different foods, according to food safety specialist Charlotte P. Brennand.[14] The FDA has approved it for many different foods, including wheat, fruit, vegetables, potatoes, flour, spices, chicken, pork, and beef. According to writer Marshall Brain, "Many people have a significant problem with the words 'nuclear radiation.'"[15] It is used most frequently in food preparation for the military, in institutions such as hospitals, and on dried spices.

BREAKDOWN IN THE FOOD CHAIN

All these ways of packaging food and keeping it fresh allow us to have plenty of food all year. We have many choices in the foods we buy. Fresh vegetables and fruits can be eaten raw. Or they can be cooked with meat or grain to make a meal. Packaged food allows us to make a meal with little effort. If time is short, a frozen dinner is ready in minutes using a microwave.

Many of these options were not available twenty or thirty years ago. Once, farms grew food for the people living only in nearby cities. People knew where their food came from. They ate what was available during specific months of the year. But then the food chain began to break down. Farmland disappeared as cities grew bigger. Farmers had to feed more people. More food was preserved and packaged so it could be eaten long after it was grown. The plants that made these foods needed raw food from farmers. Farmers had to increase crops to meet the demands of feeding people now and later. Growing food became a big business.

Today's farm machinery, such as this combine harvester, is larger and heavy. This weight can take its toll on the fields by pressing down soil and causing it to dry out.

CHAPTER 3

CHURNING OUT FOOD

WHEN WE THINK OF FARMS TODAY, WE THINK OF HUGE fields of the same crop, massive machines to plow and harvest these fields, and big business. Many people call today's farms factory farms because they seem to churn out food like factories make cars. In the United States, there are around 2.2 million farms. Most of these are still owned by families or family partnerships. This means several families working together as a company. According to a 2007 Census of Agriculture by the USDA, a mere 187,816 of the 2.2 million farms in this country accounted for 63 percent of sales of agricultural products.[1]

Whether large-scale or family partnerships, today's farmers are in business to make money. They do so by specializing. They grow only one type of crop, or they grow only those crops that are in great demand. Ranches, which raise animals for meat, also focus on one type of meat, such as beef. We now know that this method of farming has a high cost.

In the past, farms were run differently than they are today. A traditional farm included animals, called livestock. These were raised for meat, milk, or eggs. The fields included many different crops. Some were planted in different seasons or to help restore the soil. The parts of the farm interconnected. Manure from the cows was spread over the fields and plowed with the soil. This added nitrogen to the soil before planting. Animals ate corn, grass from pastures, or plant residue left after harvest, along with straw. Straw is leftover from the wheat harvest. All segments of the farm worked together like a mini ecosystem.

When traditional farmers picked their crops, they sent most to buyers. The buyers paid the farmers by weight for their crops or livestock. Then they sent the crops to stores and markets, grain to mills, and animals to butchers.

A small part of the harvest was kept for the workers on the farm. And some of it was sold at roadside stands and farmers' markets. Farmers' markets were a traditional way of selling produce. As supermarkets became more common in the 1950s, this tradition slowed down. Farmers began selling to large companies. These companies shipped the food all over the country and the world. According to organic farmer Jim Goodman, many non-farm families even stopped planting backyard gardens.[2] It was much easier to get everything they needed at the chain grocery store.

BUSINESS OF GROWING FOOD

Around this time, farming became industrialized. Big farms have become the norm, says Dr. James Horne, former Director of the agricultural division of the Environmental Protection Agency (EPA). Big farms need big equipment and high-horsepower tractors. "As they roll across the fields, their weight compacts the soil, taking out airspaces," Horne explains. This prevents the soil from holding water. So the water runs off, and the soil erodes. Compacting the soil also hurts the plant roots.[3]

Machines and large farm equipment replaced farmworkers, called farmhands. Bigger equipment allowed farmers to plant more land, which yields a larger harvest. Bigger harvests meant they could make more money. It also meant the farmers needed different methods of planting. For example, they started using fertilizer instead of manure.

These new methods fit the size and style of the bigger equipment. However, the fertilizer was more expensive. So was the bigger equipment. Now the farmer had to plant more land to get a larger crop to cover these new expenses. And larger fields meant more fertilizer and pest control. It went on and on.

As the population grew, more food was needed. This put a lot of pressure on farmers. It did not matter if the farm was small or a large company farm. The expectations for yield—how large the harvest is for a single type of crop—kept increasing. The focus became raising or growing whatever food was in demand.

MONOCULTURE FARMING

Most industrial farms specialize. They either grow crops or raise animals. Crops come from plants, and crop farms grow vegetables, grains, or fruit. They often grow only a single crop, such as soybeans, wheat, or corn. Or they grow a limited number of different crops, which are usually vegetables that are in demand. This is called monoculture farming.

Many farmers do not rotate their crops anymore. If there is a demand for corn, for example, they will grow as much as possible season after season.

The most common crops are potatoes, tomatoes, onions, salad greens, cucumbers, carrots, apples, and citrus. At the grocery store, you will see plenty of these vegetables. Other major crops in the United States today are corn, soybeans, hay, wheat, cotton, rice, and a grain called sorghum used in animal feed and processed foods.[4]

Several steps lead to a harvest. The farmer needs to get the soil ready. The soil is tilled, or the top layer is turned under. Residue from the last crop is tilled under. The standard way is using a moldboard plow, but that leaves no residue on top. Today conservation tilling leaves up to 30 percent residue. This residue is good. It helps keep the topsoil from blowing or washing away.

Herbicide is sprayed to keep weeds from growing. Grain drills and planters allow many seeds to be planted as the tractor passes over the soil.

WHAT ARE NATURAL OR ORGANIC FOODS?

As shoppers become aware of what goes into food, more want healthier choices. But those choices can feel overwhelming. What is the difference between them? No chemicals are used to grow organic foods. No preservatives are added to packaged organic food. Organic foods have labels marking them as chemical-free. Natural foods use no chemicals or preservatives in packaging. These are some of the food labels you might find on food and what each means.

USDA Organic indicates the item is 95 to 100 percent free of chemicals, pesticides, antibiotics, hormones, and synthetic additives. Packaged organic food must contain at least 70 percent organically grown ingredients.

Natural/All Natural products contain no preservatives, chemicals, or additives; ingredients may or may not be organically grown.

Cage-free/Free-range eggs or poultry products come from birds that are not kept in cages. The animals have access to open air.

Grass-fed/Open Pasture animals ideally forage for food outdoors in a pasture. The term can also mean they are fed grass while in a pen.

Pasture-raised animals roam freely outdoors and eat grass and plants.

Fair Trade Certified labels on coffee, tea, chocolate, rice, or sugar mean farmers received a fair price for their products and farmworkers were treated well and paid fair wages.[5]

After the crop begins to grow, nutrients are sprayed on plants. Nitrogen, phosphorous, and potassium are used, along with fertilizer or manure. The crops are watered and sprayed with pesticides. These chemicals keep

Free-range chickens such as these are able to roam about and are not kept in cages.

mice and insects away. Other chemicals are used to kill fungus and weeds. Finally the crop is harvested.

Most food travels long distances to reach markets. The average distance is about 1,500 miles (2,414 kilometers).[6] To prevent rotting during shipping, many fruits and vegetables are picked before they are ripe. Some ripen during transport. This happens naturally. All plants make a hormone called ethylene. It allows them to grow, mature, ripen, and age. Apples, pears, peaches, melons, bananas, tomatoes, and avocados make large amounts of it.

Ethylene can be used to ripen these fruits and vegetables if they are picked before they are ripe. This is called gassing. Fruits and vegetables are placed in a ripening room. Ethylene is piped in to trigger ripening. More is naturally produced as the food ripens. Some vegetables, such as broccoli, cabbage, cauliflower, and lettuce make only small amounts of ethylene. They are highly sensitive to it. Too much exposure can shorten the shelf life of these foods.[7]

RAISING ANIMALS FOR MEAT

Farmers who raise animals for meat are called producers. They might raise cattle to produce beef. They might raise pigs or hogs to produce pork. Poultry producers raise chickens, ducks, or turkeys. Dairy farms raise milk cows and sell the milk to dairy companies.

Some cattle ranches and dairy farms have pasture land. The animals roam and graze. The animals forage or look for food. The farmers supplement the forage with feed. Dairy farms that use this method focus on the quality of milk instead of the amount of milk. For milk producers, the higher the fat, protein, and buttermilk, the better. These are used to make cheese, yogurt, and other dairy products. A stall method is used for most milk cows. This means many cows are housed in one building. Each cow has a separate narrow stall with access to the feeding trough. The milking parlor is a similar row of narrow stalls. The cows are milked by a machine that collects and stores the milk in large tanks.

Most meat producers keep the animals together in large buildings. The temperature and lighting are controlled. Slotted floors are raised above a concrete base. This is more comfortable than standing or lying on concrete.

The fate of each animal is decided at birth. Most will become food. Some will go to a breeder house to give birth to more animals. Cattle and pigs follow similar stages. The animal is born. When it is old enough to be taken from its mother, it goes to the nursery building. This is called the feedlot for beef cows and cattle. The animals grow until they reach

On industrial farms, animals such as these pigs are kept in cages.

a specific size. Then they go to a finishing building. Here they are fed or fattened until they reach market size. For pigs, this is 240 to 275 pounds and takes five to six months.[8]

POULTRY FARMS

Eggs, chicken, and turkey meat are a healthy part of many diets today. In the early 1900s, chicken was eaten only on Sundays. Turkey was eaten on Thanksgiving and Christmas. Both are now everyday foods.

Farmers in the United States raise more than 43 billion pounds of poultry meat annually. According to the USDA Economic Research Service, about one-fifth is turkey and the rest is chicken. The United States is the top producer and exporter of poultry in the world and the second largest for eggs.[9] Chickens are raised mainly in the southern and southeastern United States. Turkeys are raised in northern states. Egg production is spread across the country.

The birds are kept inside large buildings. This protects them from weather and wild animals, which might attack the hens or spread disease. As with beef and pork production, the fate of the birds is decided when they hatch. Chickens are raised for three different functions. Each is housed on different parts of a poultry farm. Most chicks become part of the broiler flock. Broilers, or chickens under thirteen weeks old, are raised for meat. According to the US Broiler Industry, 8.6 million broilers were raised on American farms in 2009.[10] Some hens will become part of the laying flock or breeding flock. The laying flock produces eggs for market. The breeding flock lays eggs sent to the hatchery. These produce more birds for meat.

Lighting is important for the growth of chickens, ducks, and turkeys. These birds are kept in blackout houses. Artificial lighting is used to control their growth. Ducks are the fastest growing poultry birds. They will reach seven pounds in six or seven weeks. Turkeys take the longest. They are ready for market in fifteen to twenty-five weeks. That is about six months.[11]

THE IMPORTANT CYCLE OF NATURAL FARMING

Many animals are kept in livestock buildings. Farmers keep the animals healthy with antibiotics. Sometimes they are given shots or vaccines, and sometimes antibiotics are added to the feed. Some farmers give the animals hormones so they will produce more meat. This is similar to using chemicals in growing crops. The fertilizer feeds the soil, and herbicide kills weeds so plants can thrive. But do the chemicals get into the food? Does the meat contain antibiotics and hormones?

Canola and barley fields in Canada. Growing more than one crop is beneficial to the soil and results in better produce.

Many people think so. As early as the 1940s, people realized heavy use of fertilizer would damage the soil. According to agriculturist Dr. James E. Horne, one of these believers was J. I. Rodale. Rodale founded Rodale Press, the publisher of *Organic Gardening* and *Prevention* magazines. He also wrote books on organic farming in the 1940s and 1950s.[12]

Organic farming returned to the old ways of growing crops. Instead of using fertilizer, manure is used. Sometimes crops are grown simply to turn under and enrich the soil. This is called green manure and was used in Abraham Lincoln's time, explains Horne. Insects that eat other insects are used for pest control, he says.[13] Both limit chemicals.

Soil is tilled to prevent loss of topsoil. Crops are rotated in the fields. Each new crop adds to the soil, and each year the soil becomes richer. Chemicals left from industrial farming are slowly stripped away. Organic farmers also conserve water and energy. There are strict guidelines to follow if a farmer wants to be certified as an organic farmer.

THE GROWING DEMAND FOR ORGANIC

More and more supermarkets carry organic foods. Consumers now expect it. In order to meet this demand, organic farms have needed to expand. Many are larger and specialize in the crops that consumers desire. To meet the higher demand for organic foods, these farms are using some of the same methods as industrial farms, such as huge fields, specializing in certain crops, and pesticides. Of course, the pesticide is natural or approved for organic use. In a sense, they are like big green agriculture machines. What will happen years from now if these organic farms are run just like industrial farming? Will the food be of the same quality as traditional organic food?

According to environmental writer Bryan A. McCarty, "The fields must be free from [chemicals, pesticides, and man-made fertilizers] for at least three years before the farmer can harvest an organic crop. Once the three years has passed, the farmer must pay for the government-approved inspector to examine the land and declare its certification as an organic farm."[14]

When a farm wants to become certified as organic, it is a challenge. The certification process is not cheap. Also, the farm must manage to make money with food that is not yet organic and no longer cheaply grown. These costs are passed along, states Lisa Roberts, a reporter for the *Orlando Sentinel*. "The farms are also smaller. Often the harvests are smaller."[15]

Still, demand for organic foods is growing. More parents are buying organic food "to keep their children's diets free of food grown with pesticides, hormones, antibiotics or genetic engineering," states journalist Libby Quaid.[16] The toxins in foods are more dangerous for children. Children need to eat more for their size than adults. This is because their bodies are growing quickly, and so are their brains. Because they eat more food, they end up with more of the chemicals used to grow or raise that food, she says.

Roberts explains that some foods have more leftover pesticides even after washing. These are called the dirty dozen. Many people will choose organic when they buy these foods. The dirty dozen are apples, bell peppers, celery, cherries, imported grapes, nectarines, peaches, pears, potatoes, red raspberries, spinach, and strawberries. Other fruits and vegetables have low pesticide levels, says Roberts. Those include asparagus, avocados, bananas, broccoli, cauliflower, sweet corn, kiwi, mangoes, onions, papaya, pineapples, and sweet peas.[17]

It is not just what you eat. According to food writer Christie Matheson, "All those pesticides and chemical fertilizers are used to produce our juice, milk, coffee, tea, wine, and cocktails, too." Rain forests are clear-cut in order to grow coffee. This allows the sun to reach the plants so then they will grow faster. But destroying rain forests forces birds into extinction and increases greenhouse gases in the air. "Luckily, organic and shade-grown coffee is easy to find, as are organic cocoa and wine," says Matheson.[18]

Many owners of small farms use organic farming methods, but it is expensive to go through the steps to become certified as an organic grower. So many grow without chemicals or pesticides, but they don't get certified. They sell to restaurants and markets just as other farmers do. Buying from these local farmers may have an added benefit—you

An organic shade-grown coffee plantation in Mexico. Instead of cutting down trees, they are left standing so the coffee beans can be grown in a more natural environment.

are helping the local economy. But you will also be getting organic food without the added cost.

Michael Pollan, journalist and author of four food books, explains that we have shifted from the original plan for organic farming. "There were three legs to the original organic dream."[19] The first was that food was supposed to grow in harmony with nature. This meant animals were treated well. They roamed in fresh air outdoors. They ate feed but also grazed for food. No chemicals were used on plants.

TAKE ACTION!

ONE FOOD AT A TIME

It can be overwhelming to think how broken our food chain is. Making changes in our food choices can be hard. But you can begin with one food at a time. Each week swap one packaged snack for fresh food, such as carrot sticks, raisins, or an apple. Next, swap regular produce for something organic. Next, buy locally grown food or go to a farmers' market.

Buying food from local farmers has a bigger impact than you realize. It supports your community and your dollars stay local. In a sense, you are investing in that farm. Farms, according to Pollan, "produce a kind of landscape."[20] The money you spend buying locally helps conserve that landscape. Such a plan benefits in several ways. You will get more nutrients. It also impacts the environment. Less fuel is used to buy local than the produce at the grocery store.

Community newspapers often post notices for upcoming farmers' markets. They are often held on the weekends. In some areas they are set up in a parking lot. You can also find farms in your area. Look in the phone book or enter your zip code on the Local Harvest website.

The second leg was how the food came to the table. Organic food was sold through farmers' markets. People bought from local farmers. And finally, the variety of the food was large. This was the third leg. People could choose from many different kinds of apples, for instance.[21]

Pollan says that once standards were set up for organic farmers, they began to lose control of their purpose in farming naturally. The standards were thought to be necessary, he explains. In order to sell their food to big companies and get it into conventional supermarkets, some guidelines were needed. "Today the organic dream is in peril. In fact, many of the best farmers in this country no longer even use the word *organic*."[22] Today, he says, we have "organic food forced through the industrial system, shorn of its holism. What has been lost is that key insight about organic: that everything is connected. The organic dream has been reduced to a farming method."[23]

So how did it come to this? To understand, we need to return to a time just after World War II. The goal at that time was to stop world hunger. Somehow, farmers needed to find a way to produce more food and get it to the people of the world. The efforts to do this became known as the Green Revolution.

A large fruit and vegetable stall is seen here in 1928. With more Americans moving to the city, they relied more heavily on farmers to provide produce.

CHAPTER 4

FEEDING THE MASSES

THE CURRENT MODEL FOR GROWING FOOD BEGAN TO take shape early in the twentieth century. After World War I, the United States began shipping wheat to Europe and other countries. Farmers were pressed to grow more wheat and other crops. They cleared more for larger harvests. During this time, more people left the countryside to live in cities. The Roaring Twenties was going strong. People in the cities, who could not grow their own food, depended on the harvests of farmers.

One of the first hybrid crops was grown in the 1920s. It crossed two types of corn for a hardier stalk. This hybrid resisted a corn blight that had wiped out corn crops in the past.[1] People were suspicious of the man-made corn, but in time it caught on and became readily available.

The Midwest, where a majority of the farms were located, began to pay the cost for high food demands. The soil, plowed to maximize use of the fields, was eroding. A drought added to the problem, which created the Dust Bowl. To help keep the farms going, the federal government gave farmers subsidies. This is money to back the farms until harvest. They also set up programs to better use the land to stop soil erosion.

During World War II, farmers again planted to meet demands. They had to feed the troops and people overseas. Farmers worked to meet the demand for wheat, corn, fruit, and vegetables needed to feed the country. Agriculturalists, or scientists who study plants and the best ways to grow them, came up with ideas for better ways to plant crops.

Like the corn blight, wheat crops were often ruined by disease. During the 1950s, wheat rust, a type of fungus, attacked fields in the Midwest. A stronger wheat was needed that would stand up to disease.

GROWING STRONGER WHEAT

Dr. Norman Borlaug was the leading scientist in this effort. He began his work with wheat in the early 1950s. "A new race of rust destroyed more than 300 million bushels of wheat in 1954 alone," according to Leon Hesser, an agricultural economist.[2] What made this even more of a problem was wind. Wind carried the rust spores to the southern United States and Mexico. In the spring, winds carried the rust spores from Mexico north into the United States.

This type of problem is solved by crossbreeding two different types of wheat. Normally, the new variety is planted. At harvest, seeds from the best plants are used again to crossbreed. "Borlaug crossed hundreds and hundreds [of plants] because he couldn't wait the six to seven years the usual process took. He had to speed [up] the process," explained Hesser.[3]

Wheat that has been infected by rust. In the 1950s, scientists began crossbreeding wheat plants in an effort to make them stronger and more resistant to rust.

Borlaug worked on the new wheat in Mexico. The farmers he worked with had farms in two different regions. In one area, wheat grew in the summer. In the other, it grew in the winter. To speed the process, he convinced the farmers to try the new wheat in both places. Seeds were shuttled between the two locations. One was in a high altitude. The other was at sea level. The wheat grew in both places. From those harvests, Borlaug selected the best seeds. He continued crossbreeding.

This shuttle-breeding program cut the time needed to get results in half, stated Hesser.[4] Borlaug was able to grow two generations per year. The wheat was "exposed to different diseases, different soils, different climates and different day lengths," Hesser explained.[5] The wheat also grew at two different altitudes. This new wheat was not only rust resistant, but it was also highly adaptable. It grew in a range of conditions, so it would grow throughout the world.

Another result of Borlaug's work was a shorter wheat plant. Taller plants fell over when fertilizer was applied. These shorter plants did not. "Yields skyrocketed," says Hesser.[6] This meant that each crop produced much more wheat. By 1956, Borlaug had developed forty new varieties of wheat. The yield nearly doubled. This made Mexico self-sufficient in wheat production.

Borlaug also found innovative ways to crossbreed plants. In 1970, he received the Nobel Peace Prize for this work. What made his work even more remarkable is that the achievement was made in a short time. "Advances in agriculture typically are gradual," explains Hesser.[7]

STRONGER PLANTS

During this time, many countries depended on the United States to supply their corn, wheat, and other crops. During the 1960s, the goal became finding a way to help these countries feed their own people.

Farmers and scientists worked together to stop world hunger. Borlaug's work triggered a worldwide effort to increase food production in developing countries. Some scientists worked with rice and others with maize, or corn. They modeled Borlaug's work with wheat. They also did crossbreeding to create stronger plants. These stronger, healthier plants were high-yield varieties. This meant they produced a larger harvest. These high-yield varieties of corn, rice, and wheat were introduced in countries such as Mexico and India.

In the middle of the twentieth century, hunger was a problem in developing countries. Here, starving crowds in Africa line up to receive food from the World Health Organization in 1961.

Borlaug's research took place in Mexico. The subtropic weather there made many crops difficult to grow, so people in this area were hungry. This meant there was a need for high yields at harvest. These conditions helped create a type of wheat that could be grown in many places. His research produced new knowledge, and his efforts brought new technology to these farmers. They could use it on small tracts of land, as well as on large farms.

TAKE ACTION!

PROVIDE A SUSTAINABLE FOOD SOURCE

You may not be a scientist, but there is something you can do to help feed the world. Heifer International is a group that strives to end world hunger. They do this by providing sustainable food sources to families in need. When one of these families receives a cow, for example, it provides milk. The milk can be sold. This provides some income. Seeds can be planted. The plants provide food. The extra food can be sold to provide income. Seeds are collected to continue planting and benefitting from the gift of seeds. The farmers learn how to feed themselves now and in the future. These gifts are made to families or villages.

The families do not only receive the gifts. Volunteers teach them about the environment. They are taught how to keep their plot of land or animal healthy. They learn how to care for the earth. Those who receive gifts must agree to "pass on the gift." This means they give offspring of their gift to another family.[8]

Pitch in with friends or family to raise money to donate an animal through Heifer International. Visit their website to learn about sustainable living and for ideas on how you can raise money to give a gift.

The methods to create these stronger plants used newly bred varieties. These newer plants needed a lot of fertilizer. According to agricultural economist Terry L. Anderson, the use of chemical fertilizers by American farmers more than quadrupled.[9] But these new plant varieties used both water and fertilizer well. They also grew in a range of conditions. This meant the farmer was less likely to lose a crop to disease, overly rainy seasons, or overly dry seasons.

Dr. Norman Borlaug's new methods of crossbreeding wheat allowed farmers to increase productivity and grow healthier crops. Borlaug, pictured here in 1970, eventually won a Nobel Prize for his work.

In developing countries, farmers were taught different ways of farming that mimicked industrial farming in developed nations. They used fertilizer and pesticides.

"In the past forty years, hybrid grains have made modern agriculture spectacularly productive," says Horne. He points out that corn plants are uniform in height. They also form ears at the same time. Like the crops the scientists created using crossbreeding, these plants all have high yields. Horne explains, "They have been bred to respond to chemical fertilizers and have uniform growth habits adapted to farm machinery."[10]

GENETICALLY MODIFIED FOODS

Dr. Borlaug's shuttle-breeding method sped up the process for combining two species of plants. Scientists looked for other ways to speed up the process for creating hardier plants or animals. The result was bioengineered foods. Bioengineering modifies the genes of one species with those from another. For example, the genes from a wild potato that resists potato blight are placed into a potato variety grown for food. These foods are called genetically modified, or GM, foods. GM is often compared to extremely rapid selective breeding. The best traits from the hardiest plants or the healthiest animals are combined to help farmers produce more food quickly.

Genes from animals or microorganisms can be inserted into plants. This is one way plants were modified to repel certain insects and reduce the need for pesticides. Commonly grown foods, such as many varieties of squash, corn, potatoes, soybeans, and tomatoes, have been genetically modified. The FDA regulates GM foods, including genetically engineered (GE) animals. According to the FDA, "Although conventional breeding methods have been used for a long time to select for desirable traits in animals, genetic engineering is a much more targeted and powerful method of actually introducing specific desirable traits into animals."[11]

The goal of GM or GE foods is increasing the supply of food through higher yield or quicker maturity, better tasting and more nutritious food that uses fewer chemicals, and eliminating disease. For example, some milk cows are susceptible to a disease of the udder. GE results in cows that do not suffer from this blight. This creates healthier cows and higher milk production.

Many people are against GM and GE foods. They feel the risks are too high. Their biggest concern is that unexpected or harmful results could take place if modified species cross with natural species of plants or animals. According to a *Healthline* report, "Some people have raised concerns that the genes from one food that are inserted into another food may cause an allergic reaction. For instance, if peanut genes are in tomatoes, could someone with a peanut allergy react to tomatoes?"[12]

The FDA reviews scientific and safety information before deeming GM and GE foods safe for production and consumer use.

The Green Revolution did succeed in increasing food harvests. But according to organic farmer Jim Goodman, it did little for food quality. "Industrial production of the cheap food that fills our supermarkets is slowly starving us."[13] By cheap food, Goodman and other organic farmers mean that mass-production of food depletes the soil, which in turn affects the quality of the food grown in that soil. The Green Revolution tried to help farmers grow food more efficiently. It was driven by the need to protect plants and animals from disease. This led to more bountiful harvests.

Biologist and author Rachel Carson called attention to pesticides being used on crops in the 1960s. Her book on the subject, *Silent Spring*, resulted in the ban of the chemical known as DDT.

THE HISTORY OF RESISTING CHANGE

Trying to get people to make big changes is difficult. It is easier to continue doing things the way they have always been done. But scientists such as Dr. Borlaug prove change can happen. During the 1960s, another scientist forced change. Rachel Carson, a chemist, realized birds were dying. She discovered the shells of their eggs were so weak they cracked in the nest. Her research led to the book *Silent Spring*. It proved that DDT, a chemical widely used on crops and to kill mosquitoes, was the cause. She showed how "chemicals travel not only through the environment, but through food chains" and that they "can accumulate in fat tissues causing medical problems later on, and that chemicals can be transferred generationally from mothers to their young."[14] Though this led to a ban on DDT, it did not stop the use of all pesticides and other chemicals—even on our food. We use them, even knowing the long-term impact on our health. However, Carson's work did create change. We are facing the need for a similar change today.

But as farmers worked to grow more and more food to feed more and more people, they resorted to methods that organic farmers believe are hurtful in the long run. Mass production of food, in the eyes of organic farmers such as Goodman, mean a decline in food quality and a rise in scares over food safety. Both reflect poorly on food production and marketing. These failures will drive food production back to the local level. Local farmers know that healthy food comes only from healthy soil. Making the soil healthy again will produce quality food that is high in nutrition. "Local producers world-wide know that hands-on farming affords a better way to care for the soil and produce healthy food," Goodman says.[15]

Like the challenge faced by Dr. Borlaug and other scientists in the 1950s, today we face a similar dilemma. We're still trying to grow enough food to feed everyone, but the methods used are causing harm to the planet. The demand for food is expected to double in the next three decades. "One of the key challenges facing the world is to increase agricultural productivity, while reducing the environmental footprint," states the Blue Planet Prize report.[16] Current farming practices play a big role in climate change.

CHAPTER 5

HARVESTS AT RISK

THE WAY FOOD IS GROWN PLAYS A BIG ROLE IN OUR food chain. It impacts our health. It also impacts the planet. We now know that the farming machine is not working. It is not feeding everyone. There is great waste. Now we realize that it contributes to climate change on all levels: air quality, soil quality, water quality, and loss of biodiversity. Throughout the world, there is concern that if we continue this way, we will not be able to feed the growing world population. However, we already could.

"The world already produces more than 1-1/2 times enough food to feed everyone on the planet. That's enough to feed 10 billion people, the populate peak we expect by 2050," states Eric Holt Gimenez, Executive Director of the Food Trust/Institute for Food and Development Policy.[1] The problem is getting this food into the hands of the people who need it.

Too much of the food grown is lost or wasted. In the United States, more than 30 percent of food, valued at $162 billion annually, is wasted. Worldwide, enough acres of farmland to equal the size of Canada are planted but never harvested, reports environmental writer Elizabeth Royte.[2]

Food production begins with healthy soil. Farming practices need to change and improve to protect and nourish our soil.

GOVERNMENT SUBSIDIES

How is this happening? It seems the farms would go out of business if they did not profit from this much uneaten food. This waste is a result of current farming methods. A majority of farms might be owned by families or family partnerships, but they are following the lead of the roughly 3 percent of corporations that produce about two-thirds of the farm output.[3]

Whether large or small, corporate or family industrial farm, if farmers grow the right crops, they receive subsidies from the government. A subsidy is money provided to help offset expenses in an essential industry. We need food, and we need farmers to grow or raise this food. Farm subsidies began in the United States in the 1920s but became essential during the Great Depression. As part of President Franklin D. Roosevelt's New Deal program, they were supposed to be temporary, but they never stopped.

This is not only happening in the United States. According to the Blue Planet Prize report, this is happening worldwide; funds to support energy, transportation, and agriculture account for about $1 trillion. But in America, it points to a dire situation.[4] Control is in the hands of a few.

Many of those involved seem reluctant to change. Resistance most likely centers around money. But the cost of continuing in this way is not an option.

PROBLEMS WITH MONOCULTURE FARMING

Growing the same crop in huge fields or raising hundreds of animals in huge barns is the norm today. This single-crop focus, called monoculture farming, is causing harm to the planet. Crops raised this way deplete the soil of nutrients and cause erosion. "Fertilizers, rice production and [raising] livestock contribute to greenhouse gas emissions, unwise use of pesticides adds to global toxification, and fertilizer runoff plays havoc with freshwater and nearshore saltwater habitats," according to Blue Planet Prize laureates.[5]

Growth—whether plants, animals, or people—follow a natural cycle. There is a science behind this cycle. Monoculture farming tries to speed this up, often using chemicals to prevent pests (insecticides), prevent

Soil erosion can be a result of monoculture farming. The soil needs to be replenished with nutrients by rotating crops after harvesting.

weeds (herbicides), and maintain health (fungicides for plants, antibiotics for animals). The science is tweaked for better results. For example, timed lights might trick hens into laying eggs more frequently, or chemicals might be added to the soil to replace nutrients used by plants from the last harvest.

For crops, soil health is especially important. Each type of plant needs different nutrients. Unless the nutrients taken from the soil by a plant are returned, the soil eventually wears out. It is no longer fertile. Agriculturist Jim Horne compares soil to a rubber band. "A rubber band is resilient but not infinitely so. Pull on it hard for too long and it loses its elasticity."[6]

This is what too much chemical use has done to soil, he says. Farmers need to get all they can out of the land they farm. So they are forced to use methods that "may cause erosion or jeopardize the life and health of the soil in some other way."[7]

After the crop is harvested, the rest of the plant dies. It is plowed under, which adds nutrients to the soil. But it cannot add the nutrients used by the grain or vegetable that has been harvested. It can only add what is left after the harvest. Traditional farming rotated crops. Something different was grown in the plot, so the dead plant added new nutrients to the soil after harvest. This is called polyculture farming. When the same crops are grown in the same plot of soil year after year, the soil becomes worn out. This is called monoculture. Unless the depleted nutrients are added to the soil, the plant will have fewer and fewer minerals to allow it to thrive. The grain, fruit, or vegetable may still grow, but it may not be as big or taste quite as good. The yield, or amount, of each plant may be lower than the year before.

Jim Horne compares industrial farms to machines in a factory. "The machinery is ready, the routine is known, and the markets are there. But the soil is not a machine that produces crops. It is organic—alive, not dead. Monoculture depletes the soil of its life and health."[8]

Traditional farming rotated crops grown in each field. During winter, some fields might grow a winter crop, such as winter wheat. In other fields, a cover crop is grown. A cover crop is not a cash crop. It does not get harvested to add to income. A cover crop keeps the nutrient-rich topsoil from blowing away. In the spring, it gets plowed under. These plants added nutrients to the soil.

NATURAL PLANT CYCLE

Plants need nutrients from the soil. Like people, plants use these nutrients for energy and to build and maintain cells. Sunlight, air, water, and soil are all vital for plants to survive. A plant takes root in the soil. The roots take water and nutrients from the soil.

As the plant sprouts from the seed, it uses the seed pod as food. As roots take hold in the soil, the plant begins to draw on the soil for what it needs. The roots draw minerals and other nutrients from the soil into the plant. The plant uses energy from the sun. The leaves convert, or change, sunlight and carbon dioxide from the air into chlorophyll. The plant thrives. After harvest, the plant dies and is plowed into the soil. The cycle begins again. Remove any one of these elements, and the plant dies.

When so many chemicals are used in growing food, they build up in the soil. They are absorbed into young plants and added to the soil when the plant dies and is plowed under.

Conventional farming added fertilizer or chemicals to the soil to boost nutrients. "Fertilizers, it was thought, could make up for loss of fertile topsoil. The long-term effects of such farming practices have not been given enough weight or have been ignored in favor of short-term gain," according to Horne.[9] Huge equipment was used to plow and chop the topsoil. It turned the soil under, spread fertilizer, and sprayed pesticides. The goal of conventional farming is to grow more for higher yield. This is done by planting and harvesting faster. The more a farmer grows, the greater his or her profit. People all over the world depend on the farmer's good harvest. Even with all this equipment and chemical help, a lot can go wrong—too much rain, too little rain, or disease that kills or damages plants.

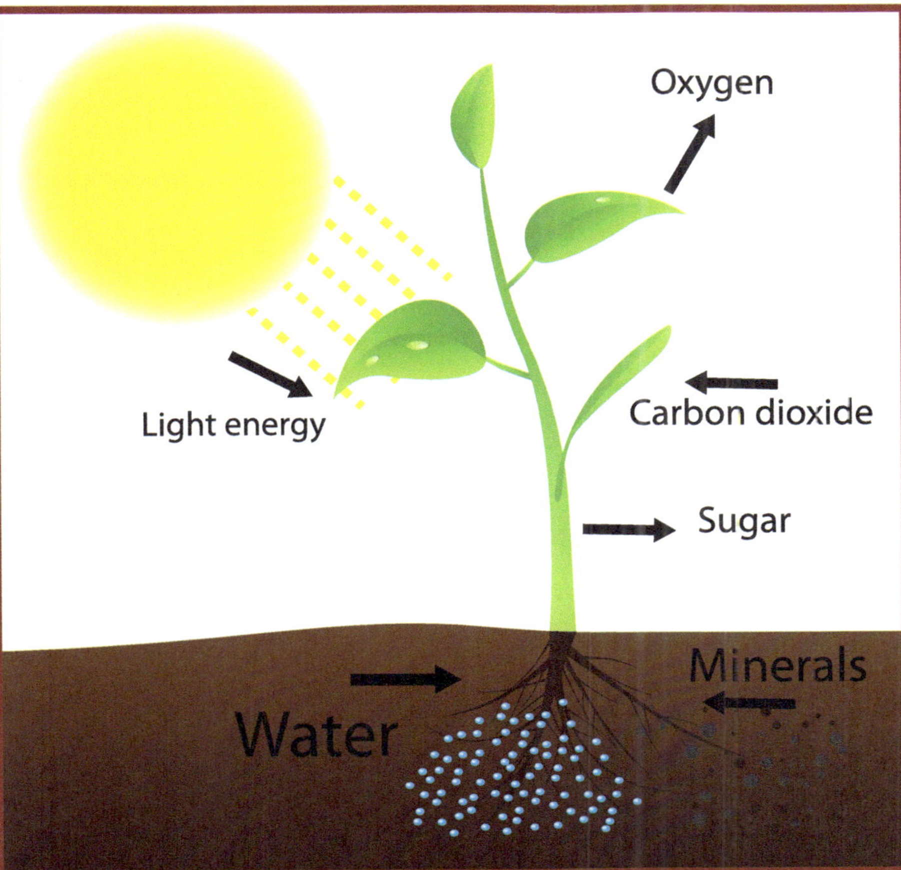

In order to grow, plants rely on sunlight and air, as well as water and minerals from the soil.

Another problem with monoculture farming is pests. Some insects harm plants, but others are beneficial. On farms raising animals for meat, too many of the same type of animals in the same space leads to disease. This might include parasites. Both disease and parasites can be easily transmitted to other animals, so antibiotics are used or added to the feed. This can happen even on farms that allow free range or grazing. It adds to the expense of raising animals for meat. Adding other types of animals improves the situation, says sustainable farmer Joel Salatin, because the traditional farm model was more symbiotic than today's.[10] This means that the different animals benefited each other. For example, chickens eating flies and larvae from cow dung stirred up the pasture as they foraged, which made nutrients more available to grazing cows.

These are just a few of the problems with industrial farming. There are others. Those play a role in climate change.

DEPLETING THE SOIL

Pressure to produce more and more food causes farmers to plow land they have not farmed in the past. Trees planted along a field are removed so that tract of land can be plowed. "Too often the shelter belts of trees, the sod waterways, the terraces, and other conservation measures proven to increase moisture and stop erosion in fields are abandoned or destroyed when a farmer deems they are cutting into his profits," says Horne.[11]

These trees are important, though. They keep the wind from drying out the ground and eroding the fields. They provide shelter to insects, birds, and animals. Many of these creatures benefit the farmer, too. They eat pests that would ruin the crop.

Where trees once stood, crops now grow in rows. "Unfortunately, this practice has been heavily supported by government programs that were designed to reduce a farmer's financial risk."[12]

A return to traditional farming helps counter this problem. Traditional farmers use methods that maintain the land. They rebuild the land. Instead of stripping trees to plant more crops, trees are planted in rows along the edges of fields. These are called shelterbelts, and they block the wind. This keeps topsoil from blowing away. This is especially important when the field is empty. Winter winds can stir up and blow away topsoil.

Farmers reduce their financial risk by sending food all over the world. Globalization of food has advantages. During winter months, we get fruit and vegetables from warmer climates. Fruits, such as kiwi, acai, and pomegranate, are available from other countries. The same is true with vegetables. But, says Goodman, globalization has disadvantages, too. The food that ends up at the supermarkets "is mass-produced by underpaid farmers and farm workers," he says.[13]

IMPACT OF WATER SUPPLY

Plants need rich soil, sun, and water to grow. Global warming can cause droughts. Droughts are periods of little rain. This dry weather hurts plants. If it does not rain often enough, farmers must water their crops. This is called irrigation. According to the Blue Planet Prize report, "70 percent of all freshwater withdrawn from rivers and aquifers is currently used for irrigation."[14] Often, water use is limited or the cost of water goes up during times of drought, so farmers cannot afford to water as much. These water shortages add to the problem. Plants that do not get enough water and are not growing in rich soil will not grow well. They may be smaller than normal, or they may not yield much at harvest.

"It is basic," says Horne. "Sun, soil, and water make life possible. Although good rich soil is becoming more difficult to find in the fields of America, water, too, is another natural resource equally at risk."[15]

David Mackay writes about agriculture and the environment. He describes water as "this liquid of life."[16] He explains that a rise in the cost of water will make food prices go up. The added cost is passed on

Farmers use a huge amount of the water supply to irrigate crops, especially during dry seasons or droughts.

to those buying the food. Also, water shortages can limit the amount of food the farmer is able to grow. "Scientific studies show that drought is occurring for longer periods and more often," he says.[17]

This is happening around the world. In the southern and western United States, Australia, and Europe, drought is devastating wheat and grain crops. Scientists are working to develop drought-resistant varieties. These would grow well with little water.

Humans who eat foods made from grain, such as bread, pasta, and cereal, are not the only ones who suffer. Some of the grain crop is used in animal feed. According to Mackay, drought has affected dairy production, especially in Australia.[18]

It does not end with the farmers and the food they grow. Water is needed for food packaging. If the water supply is limited, the company has two options. They can process less food, or they can pass the rising cost of water to those who buy the food.

Organic farmers run into these problems, too. Though their soil is healthy, crops still need water. During a drought, plants create less food to harvest. The food packing plants that make organic products also use water to process the food. A shortage means higher food prices.

GREENHOUSE GASES

All farming uses fossil fuel. It does not matter whether it is monoculture or polyculture. It does not matter whether it is organic or nonorganic. It does not matter if the farm is small or huge. All farming methods use tractors and harvesting equipment that burn fuel. Harvested crops also need to be shipped to food plants. Food packaging uses fuel to make and ship food products.

About one-fifth of fossil fuel use goes to growing, packaging, and transporting food.[19] It also creates between 19 to 29 percent of world carbon emissions.[20]

Fossil fuels create carbon dioxide. This is the number one greenhouse gas. The EPA monitors air quality and emissions. Farming falls into man-made emissions. The second most common greenhouse gas emission is methane. In farming, the main source of methane is raising animals. Cows contribute the most. They produce high amounts of methane through burps and flatulence. Their manure also releases methane. On huge beef and dairy farms, manure is collected into lagoons. It is too highly concentrated to be used for fertilizer. Also, it includes antibiotics and sometimes hormones. According to the EPA, these lagoons account for 10 percent of methane production. Because it is related to farming, this again falls into the man-made emissions category.[21]

Greenhouse gases cause global warming. Global warming leads to climate change. This impacts agriculture in several ways. Not only can climate change cause periods of drought, but warmer temperatures also affect crop growth. Some plants will die. Others will grow faster, but overall harvests could be smaller. The same occurs when climate change causes more rain. Weeds and insects multiply with both rain and warmer temperatures. In the current farming model, this requires more chemical use. But chemical use contributes to global warming.

A hog farmer stands next to a manure lagoon, where waste from the animals is collected for treatment. The methane given off from these lagoons contributes to the greenhouse gases in our atmosphere.

Since animals raised for meat eat feed crops, smaller harvests impact meat production. Warmer temperatures can also lead to more parasites and disease in animals raised for meat. They stay around longer "with earlier onset of spring and warmer winters," according to EPA reports.[22]

HIDDEN METHANE SOURCE

Agriculture contributes to global warming in so many different ways. It may be funny to think of cow burps adding to greenhouse gas emissions. But there is a hidden source of methane that is both sad and serious. All the rotting vegetables and fruit that are wasted each year create methane. During decomposition, living organisms give off methane. Landfills and Dumpsters add to the problem. While it may not compare to the large amounts coming from cows and their manure, it adds up. This is just another reason that the food chain needs to be fixed. All that food could feed millions of starving people. All that food does not have to go to waste.[23]

GENETIC DIVERSITY

The quality of the soil and the quality of the water affect how well a plant grows. But what about the plant itself? One amazing result of the Green Revolution was plants bred from only the hardiest plants. As one type of grain or tomato was crossed with another, those original varieties were lost. About 75 percent of the diversity of crops has been lost, according to the United Nations Food and Agricultural Organization.[24]

Horne argues that having many types of the same plant is important. This diversity ensures that increasing numbers of people can be fed.

The variety of plant genes provides "insurance for the future—against changes in climate, such as possible global warming, evolving pests and diseases, and changes in the availability of energy, along with changes in fashion, markets, and the structure of agriculture."[25]

The problem also occurs among animals raised for meat. The farms operate in selecting the best of the animals to use for breeding. According to Horne, they are selected to produce "a standard carcass profile, rapid weight gain, and [an] ability to utilize high-concentrate feed."[26] This ensures that the animals grow big and are ready for market quickly. Uniform sizes and shapes make the processing of the meat faster. This aids the meatpacking companies.

Any animals that do not fit this profile are not used for breeding, so their genes die out. According to the American Livestock Breeds Conservancy, about eighty breeds of cattle and pigs and many varieties of poultry are in danger of extinction.[27] The gene pool for livestock is becoming limited. Horne explains that traits that do not matter in rapid production of animals for meat are important for other types of farms. Such traits might include adaptability to different climates or a strong instinct to protect and care for their young. If animals with these traits are not bred, they become extinct.[28]

Organic farmers may not continue this selective process, but some of the species of both crops and animals are already lost. The standards for organic farming succeeded in removing chemicals and pesticides from the food we eat. But the guidelines only dealt with the manner in which food was grown or raised.

TAKE ACTION!

LIMIT MEAT INTAKE

We eat more meat than we need to be healthy. One reason is that meat producers encourage us through ads. Most of us eat meat for protein. Do we really need quarter- or half-pound hamburgers?

The amount of protein we need depends on age, gender, and body size. It also changes based on how active we are. Adults need about 0.8 grams of protein per kilogram of body weight. But children and teens need about 1.2 grams per kilogram. Most teen girls should have about 46 grams of protein per day. Teen boys should have about 52 grams per day.

Finding out how much protein you need based on weight is simple. Divide your body weight by 2.2. This gives you your weight in kilograms. Now, multiply that number by 1.2. This is how many grams of protein you need each day.[29]

Suppose you weigh one hundred pounds:

100/2.2 = 45 kg
45 x 1.2 = 54 g

You would need 54 grams of protein per day.

If you cut meat from two meals per week, you will still get plenty of protein. You also get protein from plant sources, such as nuts, nut butters, beans, lentils, and soybean products, which are used in a lot of packaged foods. Not eating as much meat can have an impact on meat producers. When we cut back on our meat consumption, they can cut back on the animals they raise. Together, this will cut back on the impact on the planet.

Many young Americans eat more meat than their bodies require. By cutting back a bit on your meat intake, you can help improve your health, as well as the planet.

According to Michael Pollan, organic guidelines overlook other important details. They relate to producing food in a way that is friendly to the environment. "There's nothing about the kind of food that may be called organic, or about distribution. There's no rule against high-fructose corn syrup. Myriad synthetics are allowed in processed organic food," Pollan says. "And we find ourselves with an organic trans-continental strawberry: 5 calories of food energy that require 435 calories of fossil-fuel to get to a supermarket near you."[30] The principles of organic farming have changed, but they need to go further. Sustainable farming is the key. We need to grow food that is healthy for people. We need to grow it in ways that are better for the earth. We need to make sure that the earth can sustain, or continue to provide, the amount of food that the world needs. This is why a New Green Revolution is needed. It is being called ever-green because it focuses on sustainable farming.

Agroecology strives to improve farming methods and make better use of the earth. Farmers plant crops, such as this buckwheat, so it can be plowed under and add nutrients back to the earth.

CHAPTER 6

EVER-GREEN AGROECOLOGY

AROUND THE WORLD, FARMERS REALIZE THE NEED to change the way we grow our food. The traditional farm was like a mini ecosystem. Crops and different animals benefited from each other. Others believe this way is too labor intensive. They see the need to fulfill a new role. As stewards of the planet, they look toward sustainable farming methods. Naomi Klein refers to this as agroecology in her best-selling book, *This Changes Everything*. Agroecology is the middle ground between industrial agriculture and local organic farming. She describes agroecology as "a less understood practice in which small-scale farmers use sustainable methods based on a combination of modern science and local knowledge."[1]

This type of farming tries to take the best of organic and industrial farming, but the methods are different. The goal is to produce the large amounts of food needed to feed the world. Wise use of machinery can make that job easier.

Agroecology has already proven successful in India, Africa, and other countries. Crop yields have doubled. It is simple and inexpensive. It also contributes to "agricultural biodiversity, health, and nutrition, and it can help to mitigate the impacts of climate change," states Ian Fitzpatrick, a researcher for Global Justice Now.[2]

"Around the world, farmers and ranchers are experimenting with a different form of agriculture, a more sustainable way of producing and distributing food and fiber," states the Sustainable Agriculture and Research Education (SARE) program.[3] James Horne describes sustainable farming as a cross between ecology and agriculture. The way the farm is run must keep up with food needs. The farm must make money, but to continue doing so, it must stay healthy. Both the farmers and the farmworkers should be treated fairly and have a good quality of life, he says. "A sustainable agriculture will yield healthy rural communities and towns, which are key to the overall health of our nation."[4]

The condition of the soil is important. So is the goal of feeding people now and in the future. Sometimes crops are grown to replenish the soil when they are turned under. Crops are rotated each year. This means that tomato plants may be grown in one field this year, but next year the field will grow squash, beans, or spinach. Chemical use is limited. If chemicals are needed to treat insects or rust, natural plant-based ones are used. Synthetic, or man-made, treatment is avoided.

LOW-INPUT HIGH-YIELD FARMING

The need for more food means farmers need to be more productive. Today, each farmer feeds 129 people in the United States and abroad. In the 1930s, each farmer fed 9.8 people.[5] Due to population increase, this is likely to double within twenty-five to thirty years. The question now is how to be more productive in a greener way. Sustainable farming is about using less fuel and fewer chemicals while producing as much food as possible.

In the United States, SARE was created to help farmers transition to sustainable farming. It encourages low-input farming. Many farmers thought this meant a return to the back-breaking labor of pre-World War II farming. That is not the case, explains Horne. Large farming equipment is still used, but its use is limited. Low-input means using fewer chemicals, which means using less fuel. When farmers are not spraying pesticides or spreading fertilizer as often, they are using less fuel because they are not running huge farm equipment as often as they used to. Many farmers are finding alternative power and fuel sources, too.

On sustainable farms, a variety of animals live together and benefit from each other.

The goal of SARE is to help farmers and ranchers increase profits. As farms prosper, so do farm families and communities. SARE also promotes environmental stewardship. The program aims to educate farmers on ways to improve soil and focus on renewable resources, such as water and fertilizer. This relates to profits. Quality soil produces healthier plants. Healthier plants produce bigger harvests. Less chemical use creates healthier soil and plants. It also saves on the costs for running the farm.[6]

Farmers and ranchers have many options for sustainable production. According to SARE, ranchers can divide rangeland into sections. They rotate where the cattle graze by moving the herd from section to section. This allows one section to recover while another is being grazed. Natural resources, such as streams and soil, are better managed.

Crop farmers can cut costs and better manage resources in several ways. Farmland is also divided into sections. Different crops are planted each season. Cover crops are used to limit weed growth and replenish the soil. They also require fewer chemicals—pesticides, herbicides, and fertilizer—which save on costs.

Fruit and vegetable growers are encouraged to sell their harvest in different ways. They might sell directly to restaurants or schools. Farmers' markets, roadside stands, and websites are other options. These support the local community, especially when local residents are able to spend their food dollars at local markets and stands.

Horne describes a wide variety of positive results from the SARE program. Use of herbicides, pesticides, and fertilizers was cut in half by cranberry growers in the Northeast. Farmers in Iowa devised a new way to till or plow the soil. It is called ridge tillage, and it controls erosion. It also requires less fuel for plowing and fewer chemicals. In Florida, researchers found organic pest control options. They will reduce the exposure to pesticides many farmworkers have. They could also save growers about four hundred dollars per acre. Fruit and vegetable producers in Connecticut now supply Hartford schools with fresh produce. This provides new markets, but it has another bonus. Inner-city children get high-quality fresh food and also learn about nutrition and the environment. They participate in farm field days and cooking demonstrations by chefs.[7]

CONTROL OF BIG BUSINESS

To make changes to the food chain, we will need to get big business to change. "Today, six companies control 60% of the world's commercial seed market, and ten fertilizer companies account for more than 40% of their global market. The largest four traders control around 90% of global grain," says Ian Fitzpatrick.[8] A power grab is taking place among governments, huge corporations, donors, and development agencies. Some are even going green. They have realized that there is big money in organic farming. They even support environmental protection groups—not for the benefits to the planet but for the money they can make. Part of the sustainable movement's goal is to return the power to the millions of people who produce, buy, and consume food. "Fundamentally," states Fitzpatrick, "agroecology is about shifting the way our food system—land, seeds, markets, and labor—is controlled by big business."[9] It will not be easy. But it has been done in the past, and it can happen again.

RESTORING SOIL NUTRIENTS

Agroecology involves methods that work to restore nutrients to the soil but also allow the soil to retain nutrients. Planting trees and shrubs in crop and livestock fields and using green manure or quick-growing plants to prevent erosion and replace lost nutrients are a few examples. So is intercropping. This means planting two or more crops near each other to maximize light, water, and nutrients. "These methods and many others maintain healthy soil while producing nutritious food—more than industrial agriculture does, per unit area—and limit the need for farmers to buy expensive products like chemical fertilizers, and patented seeds," explains Klein.[10]

Another way to restore soil is using fertilizer trees, according to M.S. Swarthe in a report for the Blue Planet Prize. He described how dryland farming in India is meeting with success. Using fertilizer trees, water harvesting ponds, and a biogas plant in every farm improved productivity

An African woman checks the corn crop on a small farm. Scientists have introduced new farming techniques in Africa, including planting trees to enrich the soil.

and profits.[11] A Cuban-born soil scientist, Pedro Sanchez, also proved this method to be effective. He won the World Food Prize in 2002 for the work he did to replenish poor soil in Africa. According to journalist Elizabeth Weise, in 2002 in sub-Saharan Africa, about 180 million people did "not know where their next meal [was] coming from."[12] The soil in Africa is shallow. During many years of farming, it had lost its nutrients. Nitrogen was especially lacking. Conventional farming adds nitrogen using fertilizer. This method is expensive in Africa. It costs 200 to 600 percent more to buy fertilizer there than anywhere else in the world. Another way was desperately needed.

Sanchez and his colleagues came up with a plan that took conditions in Africa into account. "At the beginning of [the] rainy season, farmers interplant corn—a dietary staple—with local varieties of fast-growing trees that can take nitrogen from the air by using bacteria in their roots," explains Weise.[13]

At first, the trees grow very slowly. Around the time the corn is ready for harvest, the trees hit a growth spurt. They can grow up to nine feet in eight months. They are allowed to grow for the crop season. This takes a full year. "Just before the next planting cycle, when the rains are ready to begin, the farmers cut down the trees. The leaves are dug into the soil. Doing this can add 247 to 494 pounds of vital nitrogen to each acre of soil," says Weise.[14] The wood from the trees is used for firewood. Wood from four-fifths of an acre is enough for one family for one year, she explains. This protects against deforestation.

But there are two more parts to Sanchez's plan. In addition to nitrogen, African soil needs phosphorous. Africa has many deposits of rock phosphates. These are rocks that contain the mineral phosphorous. Fertilizer companies have ignored these deposits because they are too small to collect profitably. But small farmers can collect these rocks, crush them, and add them to the soil. The acidity that occurs naturally in the soil helps break down the rock. This creates a form of phosphorous the soil can use. Next, farmers gather a weedy shrub called Mexican sunflower, whose leaves contain many nutrients. It grows along roadsides and along farm boundaries from Ethiopia to South Africa. Farmers chop the stems and leaves into small pieces. They place them at the bottom of planting holes along with the seed. "This provides micronutrients for healthy growth," states Weise.[15]

When such simple methods are matched to the conditions of the farm environment, crop yield can double or quadruple. It also gives farmers a chance to grow other types of crops.

IMPACT OF FUEL IN GROWING FOOD

Fuel has a big impact on food at nearly every stage. Fuel is used to grow the food we eat. According to the SARE program, the majority of energy used in farming comes from using fertilizers, herbicides, pesticides, and other chemicals. Many are derived from fossil fuel or fuel processing. "Reducing the use of these materials, especially nitrogen fertilizer, is an effective way to cut back energy use on the farm," SARE says. If a farmer uses manure instead of nitrogen, he would save around eighty-five dollars per acre. More significantly, he would save forty thousand cubic feet of natural gas.[16] When less fuel is used, it pollutes the air and water less, too.

One major concern with the food system is specialized farms. Crops, which need fertilizer, are grown miles away from ranches and meat producers. Raising animals for meat requires grain and high-protein feed. But the farms that produce it are miles from the ranches. The livestock

Fruit that has fallen on the ground can be distilled and made into high-octane fuel.

generates huge quantities of manure, but there are no fields on which to spread it. It could be shipped to crop land, but it is heavy. It would burn a lot of fuel to get it there. So, it becomes a pollutant. Farmers growing crops end up using chemical fertilizers instead. "As much as forty percent of energy used in the food system goes towards the production of artificial fertilizers and pesticides," according to Sustainable Table, a group that promotes sustainable agriculture.[17]

Farmers and ranchers are finding ways to cut back on fuel use. The SARE program has helped. Different farming methods require less fuel. But farmers are finding alternatives, too. They are using clean energy. Fruit left after harvest is collected and distilled. This creates clean-burning, high-octane fuel to run farm equipment. Some farmers are growing crops just to use in making their own fuel. Corn ethanol is an example. Others use animal waste, according to SARE.[18] Selling surplus fuel is a source of added income for some farm families.

Other efforts to streamline farm production also boost profit by saving money. For example, through the SARE program, farmers are using solar panels to heat greenhouses. They are also replacing old lightbulbs with energy-efficient ones. Still other farmers are harnessing wind energy and using improved irrigation methods. These are all sources of clean energy and solutions for streamlining farm production.

One fuel impact that still needs to be addressed is shipping food. Even organic or sustainably grown food needs to be shipped. Often this distance is great. According to environmental writer Christie Matheson, "Given that food travels on average of 1,500 miles [2,414 km] before it lands on your plate, eating locally has the edge when it comes to using less transportation energy."[19]

It is common to ship food not only across the country but across borders. Some is shipped overseas. "In 2005, more than $120 billion of agricultural products crossed US borders as imports and exports," states Sustainable Table.[20] This is not good because of the energy used on shipping. This is still one part of the food chain that needs to be fixed.

THE FUTURE OF FARMING?

Correcting the food system and farming methods is important. But we also need to look to the future. Twenty or thirty years from now, we do not want to run into another food crisis, states Cornell University Professor Rebecca Nelson.[21] She describes genetic enhancement, new biofuels, and smart fertilizer as blending science with agriculture. Some call this new approach to farming smart breeding. It may point to the future. It takes the idea of genetic modification, or GM, to a new level. It could be called the new and improved GM crop, and it is destined to put genetically modified crops out of business.

Genetic modification develops new varieties by inserting genes from a desired animal or plant into an organism. Sometimes DNA from a plant is used to replace DNA in an animal cell. Sometimes animal DNA is added to plant DNA. For example, rather than having to spray pesticides to keep an insect from ruining a crop, GM can add an element from another plant or organism to keep the pests away. Antibiotics or vitamins can also be included through GM so food is more nutritious. But combining the DNA of animals or organisms with plants raises fears for many people.

The FDA has found GM foods to be perfectly safe. In fact, most people have probably eaten GM foods many times without being aware of it. The

FDA does not require these foods to be labeled. However, organic foods are not allowed to be genetically modified.

However, smart breeding is a new technique. According to science writer Anastasia Masurat, it can "radically improve crops without inserting genes from other organisms."[22] It promises to outdo GM because the science has moved on, says Masurat. GM causes fears about food safety and corporations controlling seed stock.

Smart breeding blends the past and the future. It applies the age-old method of crossbreeding with technology. Precise genetic mapping is used to find two varieties to crossbreed. Smart breeding selects specific traits, such as drought resistance, a certain color, or a specific taste. "The dormant genes for many desired traits have been found hiding in rare or wild varieties of some plants. Smart breeders employ crossbreeding techniques to draw out these traits," Masurat explains.[23]

A researcher at a lab that produces genetically engineered seeds tests spinach for disease. While genetic modification is a controversial topic, new advances have resulted in safer ways to produce healthier food.

Farmers have been crossbreeding plants and animals for hundreds of years—perhaps even longer. They learned to breed the strongest to ensure hardy stock or plants that produced more. Sometimes good outcomes arose out of simple luck, and new varieties of plants were the result. Now, scientists are able to use precise information about the plant. They

TAKE ACTION!

LOCAL FOOD BANKS

The Green Revolution set out to feed the world. Agroecology seeks ways to rely on renewable resources. You can be a renewable resource in your community, too. Organizations that feed the hungry are always in need of donations. You can do more than donate money or food, though. You can give back to your community by helping at a food bank or volunteering at a soup kitchen or homeless shelter.

Your task as a volunteer might be to box food to give to those in need, or, you might make or serve food at a shelter. You might also help with food drives. These are charitable organizations, and they depend on food donations.

Another way you could help is to locate food sources. For example, there are groups who volunteer at farms after harvest. They gather food left behind during harvest. They also gather fruits and vegetables that are discarded. They might have imperfections, so they are rejected by food buyers. Food banks and shelters will take them.

You could also work with local restaurants or grocery stores to pick up food they would throw out at the end of the day. Finally, if your yard or a neighbors has a fruit or nut tree, they might welcome someone helping to pick the fruit before it falls off or rots. In some cities there are charities that will harvest this fruit. This helps the homeowner, as well as people depending on local charities for food.

can look to the role each gene plays in a plant's makeup. Crossbreeding can take years. This was one of the reasons that Borlaug came up with shuttle-breeding—to speed up the process. In a lab, smart breeding can speed up the results. "Without genetic modification's expense, patent politics, or potential environmental risks, smart breeding is the best of both worlds," explains Masurat.[24]

A lot can be done with smart breeding techniques. A lot has already been done. Researchers in West Africa created rice that resists disease and drought. American scientists are working on corn plants that turn red when they need water. It is hoped that these new crops will solve hunger and nutrition problems throughout the world.

These crops of the future have been dubbed superorganics. According to Masurat, "ideally they'll be tasty and safe and won't need as much pesticide, fertilizer, and water."[25] They will please everyone—those who eat them, those who grow them, and those who monitor our food and its impact on the environment.

These smart foods, or superorganics, might be the future of sustainable farming. They build on the changes farmers are making to ensure that the land can sustain feeding the world for generations. They draw from the success of the first Green Revolution and move food production into the future. But this is still only part of the cycle for sustainable farming. There are other parts that fit into the cycle, including those who eat the food.

CHAPTER 7

FIXING THE FOOD CHAIN

WE NOW KNOW THAT ENOUGH FOOD IS ALREADY grown to feed the world. So why are so many of us starving? Even one child going hungry over the weekend is one too many. Why are so many of us overfed yet undernourished? And why is so much food wasted each year? The answers point to broken links in the food chain. This food chain includes many links: those who grow the food, those whose ship it, those who package and prepare it, those who sell it, those who buy it, and those who eat it.

The problem may seem too overwhelming for teens to worry about. But teens have clout when it comes to food. They spend a lot of money on food and have a say in more than 80 percent of their family's food buying decisions. Advertisers know this. Otherwise, they would not track teen spending—$16.4 billion on food each year.[1]

Teens can take an active role in helping to fix a broken food system. One way is becoming aware of what they eat. Another is choosing wisely

Farmers' markets are a great way to get fresh, healthy food while supporting local farms.

where and how they spend their money on food. It is like a vote—for or against—how food is grown and gets into their hands.

WE EACH PLAY A ROLE

Sustainability is not a job only for farmers. Those of us who eat the food have a responsibility, too. It is important to think about how land, water, and air work together. Pollution of soil, water, and air affects plants. How much water is available is also a factor. During times of drought, water use is restricted. When people do not adhere to those restrictions, it further limits water available for farming.

Food packing plants use a lot of water and fuel to make easy-to-prepare foods. About a quarter of the energy needed to get food from field to table is used in food processing and packaging, according to Sustainable Table Web. Once food is processed it must be heated or cooked at home. This uses even more energy. You can help cut this use by avoiding processed foods. Buy fresh food. Choose foods with less packaging. Cut back on how much meat you eat. "Meat is the least fuel-efficient food we have," states Sustainable Table.[2]

We may at first find it difficult to have to think so much about the food we eat. What does it contain? What do we know about that food? How was it grown? How far away was it grown? We may miss the convenience of old ways—berries available all year long instead of only during summer, and plenty of choices from globally available food. But knowledge about that food and how it was grown and processed may cancel out the ease of buying it. "Change for the better is seldom easy, but always worth it," says Jim Goodman.[3]

THE HIGH COST OF INACTION

The way food is currently raised is not working. The cost—to our health and in the number of people going hungry—is too high. The need to act is urgent. Advances in science and technology should improve life. Instead, one in three children born in 2000 or after will develop Type 2 diabetes. For the first time in history, today's generation will have a shorter life expectancy than their parents. This is going backward instead of advancing. Plus, the cost of hunger and food insecurity to the US economy is $167 billion per year.[4] Not only is our farming model creating climate change and causing global damage, it is also hurting the people it is supposed to feed.

TEENS GOING CLEAN AND GREEN

More and more teens are getting involved in understanding about food. They are choosing to eat clean. This means eating food that is whole and fresh—grown without harmful chemicals and raised in a way that helps sustain the environment. With one in four schools now using school gardens to teach science and food health, many teens have experienced growing food. They have tasted freshly picked vegetables. They know the variety is far greater than produce sections at the grocery store, and they are getting interested in agriculture. Some even choose to spend their summer learning more about growing and preparing fresh food.

Imagine heading to camp for the summer. But at this camp, you grow and eat organic vegetables and brew biodiesel fuel. You might also build a habitat to help save threatened wildlife. Some of the teens at this camp choose to teach programs that share eco-friendly living tips with area children. It is a summer camp, so typical camp activities are part of the program, too. Plan on going horseback riding, swimming, hiking, and rock climbing.

Longacre Farm is a 225-acre (91-hectare) organic farm in Newport, Pennsylvania. Solar panels provide energy, and the teens who go to the camp learn to become stewards of the earth. After their summer experiences, they leave with a new understanding about "the world's ecological balance, and green alternatives to implement back at home and in their classrooms," says Susan Smith, Director of the Longacre Leadership Program. A total of seventy-two young people aged twelve to eighteen attended this international program in 2007.[5]

This is one way to explore sustainable living. Now you can also have a career in this area. EcoGastronomy is a major that was launched by the

First Lady Michelle Obama teaches a group of young people how to harvest a vegetable garden. There are many ways for you to get involved in the green food movement, from making better food choices to planting your own garden.

University of New Hampshire. Students combine the EcoGastronomy major with nutritional science courses in this degree program. "We are seeing growing student interest in food and sustainability and an eagerness to understand and connect with the local, regional and global food system," says Joanne Curran-Celentrano, Professor of Nutritional Sciences at the University of New Hampshire and cofounder of the program.[6] Students learn how to grow and prepare foods. They work on solutions to the challenges of growing food. Social justice in the food system is another issue they explore. They get experience working at the organic research farm and working with Local Harvest in the university's dining service. Many want to be chefs or caterers or go into the hospitality industry.

COMMUNITY AND URBAN FARMS

As people become more aware of how food is grown and packaged, many seek alternatives. However, those choices are limited in urban areas. There is little space to grow your own food, and getting fresh food other ways is difficult—at least until recently.

A new type of farming is emerging. It is happening in urban areas, so it is called urban farming. The city of Albuquerque, New Mexico, has an example of urban farming. It has been a part of life in Albuquerque for a long time. Dan Schuster, who manages Rio Grande Community Farms, told journalist Heather Clark, "We're so far behind, we're ahead!" As the rest of the country built up, people in Albuquerque continued growing their own food. "The rural lifestyle of backyard horse stables, fresh eggs for breakfast, fruit trees and vegetable gardens that people take for granted in many Albuquerque neighborhoods is catching on around the country," states Clark.[7]

It is catching on in other cities, too. Urban Farming, a nonprofit group in Detroit, Michigan, turns vacant lots into gardens. The group started with three gardens in 2005 and had six hundred three years later. They have since expanded into cities such as New York, St. Louis, Chicago, Atlanta, Minneapolis, and New Orleans, according to Clark. Will Allen, a retired professional basketball player, started Growing Power in 1993. Based in Milwaukee, it makes fresh produce available to about ten thousand people in the area. "Many live in the city's poorest neighborhoods where supermarkets are few and far between," according to SARE, which shares some of Allen's urban gardening ideas with others. Allen took one acre of poor-quality inner city land and transformed it into an urban garden. It produces $200,000 worth of produce per year. Allen credits

Don’t have a lot of space? Look into starting a vertical garden like this one in Los Angeles. It is a perfect solution for urban areas that have limited room.

compost and worms for replenishing the soil. Growing Power collects organic waste from city businesses for composting. Allen says, "We've got to grow new soil. Not just little bits but hundreds of yards of soil if we're going to grow this urban food revolution, because we can't grow it in the existing soil."[8] They do this by collecting one hundred thousand pounds of organic waste per day. Aquapods, or pools for raising fish, also serve to water the plants. Water from these pools and fish waste fertilize the plants. The water is circulated back to the aquapods. Growing vegetables in columns filled with dirt is another way urban farms make use of limited space. This is called vertical gardening.

The urban farm doesn't stop with community gardens, explains Clark. Farmers have often brought organic produce into farmers' markets, restaurants, and schools so people could taste the difference compared to what they usually eat. Now, local farmers who use commercial farming practices are also "choosing to plant vegetables based on nutritional value and taste, rather than making decisions based on a business contract or how long a vegetable can sit on a shelf," says Clark.[9]

COMMUNITY-SUPPORTED AGRICULTURE

Sometimes people in the community pledge to help cover the cost of running a local farm. This is called community-supported agriculture (CSA). Each member who pledges support also shares in both the risks and benefits with the farmer. Throughout the year, members receive shares, or some of the harvest from the farm.[10] This food changes with the season and harvest.

The food is fresher. This means your body gets to use more of the nutrients. Eating locally also saves fuel. The food is not shipped to food packing plants and then to the grocery store. Michael Pollan says, "When you buy

Try getting involved in a community garden in your area or create your own. You will meet other people who care about the food supply, learn about gardening, and help the earth.

local you're voting for a short, highly legible food chain—one that supports all three legs of the original vision. The shorter food chain brings consumer and producer together, and the producer gets to tell her story."[11] You get to know the farmer. You know where the food came from and how it was grown. Farmers' markets and local farms also sell eggs, milk, and hothouse greens in winter. "With every food purchasing decision, we are helping to create the world we want to live in, one bite at a time," says Pollan.[12]

Growing enough food to feed the world is a big responsibility. It requires farmers to become stewards of the earth so the soil and land will still be able to grow or raise enough food to feed people years from now. But farmers need the commitment of everyone who eats the food, too. We must all work together.

TAKE ACTION!

START A SCHOOL OR COMMUNITY GARDEN

If your school or community does not have a garden, why not get one started? In schools, students do the work in the school garden. The work of overseeing a school farm can be shared by health, science, and even economics teachers. Students see the plants at every stage and learn about how they grow. They recognize the raw form of foods. This makes it easier to find, buy, and add vegetables to their diets. They also learn about health and nutrients from each plant. Most school gardens also give the produce to their school cafeterias and sell it to local restaurants or at farmers' markets.

Community gardens focus on groups of neighbors helping to plant, water, weed, and harvest fruits and vegetables. Some programs provide a plot to be worked. Others turn it into a group effort with harvest divided among those involved. Excess is given to food banks, shelters, or other charities. Or it might to given to other neighbors to encourage their participation in the garden.

Many programs exist to help people get started with a community garden, including Allen's Growing Power. The EPA also has an urban agriculture division. Its mission is to create sustainable use of brownfields, or vacant land. The USDA has a website called LetsMove.gov that has information on starting school gardens. Another helpful group for school gardens is KidsGardening.org.

To be a steward of the earth, you first need to become a steward of your body. Change begins with choices. Understand what your body needs to be healthy. Select foods that support your body, such as eating more whole, fresh foods that will benefit you. This is easier to do when you support local farmers. Finally, reach out in your community to make sure the hungry are fed. You can do something now through these small choices. Become a steward of your own health and that of the earth by thinking about where your food came from and how it will benefit you.

APPENDIX

Excerpts from "Environment and Development Challenges: The Imperative to Act," a joint paper by the Blue Planet Prize laureates, presented February 20, 2012:

FOOD SECURITY

We theoretically could feed the world today with affordable food while providing a viable income for the farmer, with appropriate distribution of what is harvested. But with business-as-usual this will not occur in the foreseeable future. Most of today's hunger problems can be addressed with the appropriate use of current technologies, particularly appropriate agro-ecological practices (e.g. no/low till, integrated pest management, and integrated natural resource management), but these must be coupled with decreased post-harvest losses, and broad-scale rural development. This will require recognizing the critical role of women and empower[ing] them through education, property rights, access to financing, and access to markets using improved roads. There is also a need to negotiate and implement global-scale trade policy reforms to stimulate local production in developing countries.

Emerging issues such as climate change and new plant and animal pests may increase our future need for higher productivity and may require advanced biotechnologies, where the risks and benefits need to be carefully evaluated.

To impart the dimension of economic and ecological sustainability in farming requires promotion of an integrated attention to conservation, cultivation, consumption and commerce. A country can become a knowledge and innovation super-power only if it pays attention to nutrition and education for all children, women and men from conception to cremation.

INNOVATION AND GRASS ROOT ACTION

The Earth has enough for everyman's need
but not for one man's greed

— GANDHI

At the outset it must be said since Rio 1992 community based groups in the poorer most inaccessible rural areas around the world have demonstrated the power of grass roots action to change policy at regional and national levels. In consultation with communities, innovative methods and approaches have been put into practice and indeed been scaled up to cover thousands of individuals living in communities on less than $1/day.

But sadly they have not been collectively visible enough to catch the eyes of the policy makers and the movers and shakers who are formulating crucial global policies without engaging with them at the cutting edge levels.

Without devaluing the tremendous contribution of such grass roots action and while showing them the respect and recognition they deserve there is an urgency now to bring them into mainstream thinking, convey the belief all is not lost, and the planet and humanity can still be saved.

New ideas have been put into practice as a result of collective grass roots action where lessons can be learnt if only we have the humility and ability to listen. The main lessons learnt could be summarized:

- There is no urban solution to the basically rural problem of poverty. The simple solutions of how the rural poor have tackled the issues of climate change and water security already exist but we have yet to put a mechanism in place to learn from them. There are best practices with potential to scale up that needs to be highlighted.
- The answer to addressing the critical issues of poverty and climate change is not primarily technical but social. The problems of corruption, wastage of funds, poor technology choices and absent transparency or accountability are social problems for which there are innovative solutions emerging from the grass roots. For instance, the idea and practice of Public Hearings and Social Audits came from the people who were fed up with government inaction in India. Now it has been institutionalized and is benefitting nearly 600,000 villages in India.
- Grass roots groups have found the value and relevance of a South-South Partnership where the use and application of traditional knowledge, village skills and practical wisdom between communities across Continents have resulted in low cost community based solutions that have had an incredible impact in improving the quality of life. Migration from rural to the urban areas has decreased. Dependency on urban and technology skills has decreased.

- The empowerment of women is the ultimate sustainable rural solution. By improving their capacity and competence to provide basic services in the rural areas . . . they could be the new role models that the world is looking for.
- The long term answer is not a centralised system but a demystified and decentralized system where the management, control and ownership of the technology lie in the hands of the communities themselves and are not dependent on professionals, with little relevant experience, from outside the villages.
- Listen and learn how poor communities all over the world see the problems of energy, water, food and livelihoods as inter-dependent and integrated as part of a living eco system and not viewed separately.

To read the paper in its entirety, go to:
http://www.af-info.or.jp/en/bpplaureates/doc/2012jp_pr_en.pdf.

Excerpts from "Climate Change and Hunger: Responding to the Challenge," World Food Programme, 2009:

INTRODUCTION

Climate change is one among a range of risks affecting the food security of poor people and developing countries. The effects of climate change are not always easily discernable from the effects of other risks, particularly because the indirect consequences of climate change—such as those affecting livelihoods, health and migration—have the greatest impact on poor people.

Accordingly, the challenge of adapting to climate change in terms of food security and other sectors is far from being a stand-alone area of activity. On the contrary, the central requirements are to mainstream adaptation in national development programmes and to focus on ways of replacing vulnerability with resilience. This part of the report discusses ways of achieving this aim in the context of agriculture and access to food, focusing on the contribution that social protection systems can make to building resilience to climate change. The chapter concludes with a discussion of the institutional reform requirements implied by this agenda at the national and international levels.

CLIMATE CHANGE IN THE WIDER RISK CONTEXT

The need to adapt to climate change will be a fundamental driver of developments in agriculture, food security and work to achieve the Millennium Development Goals (MDGs). But the challenge posed by climate change is just one of a range of risks that affect agriculture and food security in developing countries.

Economic volatility, for example, has had a clear impact on food insecurity in developing countries over the last two years. Before the beginning of the food and fuel price spike in the summer of 2008, the global total of undernourished people was estimated at 854 million (United Nations High-Level Task Force on the Global Food Crisis, 2008). The World Bank estimates that between 73 and 105 million more people became poor between 2005 and 2007 as a result of increases in food prices (World Bank, 2008b). Yet even after food prices fell sharply from the summer of 2008 onwards and as the global economic downturn gathered pace, the disproportionate exposure of poor people to the effects of the downturn meant that the number of undernourished people continued to increase. By July 2009 the global total of undernourished people surpassed 1 billion for the first time (FAO, 2009).

Competition for land is another significant resource scarcity risk in the global food security outlook. Even before the impacts of climate change are taken into account, FAO and the United Nations Environment Programme (UNEP) estimate that 16 percent of the world's productive land is already degraded (FAO/UNEP, 1997). Climate change will not only lead to further land degradation or desertification: it will reduce land availability because climate mitigation strategies—for example avoided deforestation, afforestation as a means of sequestering carbon dioxide, and biofuel production—require land that might otherwise be used for food production. Further sources of demand for land include fibre production for paper, demand for timber and the world's growing cities, which tend to be sited on the best agricultural land (FAO, 2006; World Bank, 2008a; Buringh and Dudal, 1987).

To read the report in its entirety, go to:
http://documents.wfp.org/stellent/groups/public/documents/newsroom/wfp212536.pdf.

CHAPTER NOTES

Introduction: High Alert! Food Crisis

1. Ross Toro, "Americans Eat Nearly a Ton of Food Per Year (infographic)," *LiveScience.com*, January 23, 2012, http://www.livescience.com/18070-food-americans-eat-year-infographic.html.

2. Julie Bizzozero, "U.S. Teens Spend $16 Billion on Food Annually," Trending Food, May 14, 2014, foodproductdesign.com/blogs/trending-foods/2014/05/u-s-teens-spend-16-billion-on-food.aspx.

3. Robert Bates, *Ingredients*, Center for Independent Documentary (New York: New Video Group, 2011).

4. Elizabeth Royte, "One-Third of Food Is Lost or Wasted: What Can Be Done," Future of Food, *National Geographic*, October 12, 2014, http://news.nationalgeographic.com/news/2014/10/141013-food-waste-national-security-environmental-science-ngfood/.

5. Bates.

6. Tom Karst, "CDC Report Grades Students Poorly on Produce Consumption," *The Packer*, November 28, 2011, http://www.thepacker.com/fruit-vegetable-news/CDC-report-grades-students-poorly-on-produce-consumption-134611753.html.

7. Timothy B. Wheeler, "Lake Clifton Greenhouse Project Harvest 1st Crops," *Baltimore Sun*, December 17, 2009, http://www.baltimoresun.com/features/green/bal-md.gr.hoophouse17dec17,0,601643.story.

8. "National Overview: Bringing the Farm to School," The Farm to School Census, Food and Nutrition Service of the United States Department of Agriculture, accessed June 27, 2015, http://www.fns.usda.gov/farmtoschool/census#.

9. Lori Silverbush, *A Place at the Table: the Crisis of 49 Million Hungry Americans and How to Solve It* (Los Angeles: Magnolia Pictures, 2013).

10. "Prevalence of Childhood Obesity in the United States, 2011–2012," Centers for Disease Control and Prevention, http://www.cdc.gov/obesity/data/childhood.html.

11. Bates.

12. Jean-Paul Jaud and Gabriel Yared, *Food Beware: The French organic revolution* (First-Run Features, 2009).

Chapter 1: Fuel Up With Food

1. The Prevention Institute, "The Facts on Junk Food Marketing to Kids," *Institute of Medicine*, accessed July 21, 2015, http://www.preventioninstitute.org/focus-areas/supporting-healthy-food-a-activity/supporting-healthy-food-and-activity-environments-advocacy/get-involved-were-not-buying-it/735-were-not-buying-it-the-facts-on-junk-food-marketing-and-kids.html.

2. "Hunger Statistics," United Nations World Food Programme, 2015, http://wfp.org/hunger/stats.

3. "Hunger and Poverty Fact Sheet," Feeding America, 2015, http://www.feedingamerica.org/hunger-in-america/impact-of-hunger/hunger-and-poverty/hunger-and-poverty-fact-sheet.html.

4. "Child Hunger in Canada: A Growing Hunger," *Breakfast for Learning*, 2013, http://breakfastforlearning.ca/how-to-help/child-hunger.

5. National Center for Health Statistics, "Prevalence of Childhood Obesity in the United States 2011-2012," accessed June 27, 2015, *Centers for Disease Control*, http://www.cdc.gov/obesity/data/childhood.html.

6. Childhood Obesity Foundation, "Statistics," April 2015, http://childhoodobesityfoundation.ca/what-is-childhood-obesity/statistics/.

7. "About BMI for Children and Teens," Centers for Disease Control and Prevention, accessed March 3, 2010, http://www.cdc.gov/healthyweight/assessing/bmi/childrens_BMI/about.htm.

8. Steven Dowshen, "Metabolism: A Body Basics Article," *Kidshealth*, 2, accessed June 29, 2015, http://kidshealth.org/parent/general/body_basics/metabolism.html.

9. Cheryl Redmond, "Eat Your Vitamins," *Body + Soul* magazine, August 2008, 88.

10. Ann Burgess and Peter Glasauer, *Family Nutrition Guide* (Rome, Italy: Food and Agriculture Organization of the United Nations, 2004), 14.

11. Jim Goodman, "We Need to Eat Locally Again," *The Cornucopia Institute*, August 4, 2008, www.cornucopia.org/2008/08/we-need-to-eat-locally-again.

12. Redmond.

Chapter 2: Packaged for Ease and Appeal

1. "FAO's role in food loss and waste," Food and Agriculture Organization of the United Nations, 2015, http://www.fao.org/food-loss-and-food-waste/en/.

2. Elizabeth Royte, "One-Third of Food Is Lost or Wasted: What Can Be Done," Future of Food, *National Geographic*, October 12, 2014, http://news.nationalgeographic.com/news/2014/10/141013-food-waste-national-security-environmental-science-ngfood/.

3. Eric Schlosser, *Fast Food Nation* (New York: Houghton Mifflin Company, 2001), 173.

4. "Slaughterhouses and Processing," *Sustainable Table*, accessed June 30, 2015, http://www.sustainabletable.org/279/food-processing-slaughterhouses.

5. Ibid.

6. "Overview of Food Ingredients, Additives, & Colors," FDA/IFIC Brochure, U.S. Food and Drug Administration, April 2010, 5, http://www.fda.gov/Food/IngredientsPackagingLabeling/FoodAdditivesIngredients/ucm094211.htm.

7. Nutrient Data Laboratory, "USDA Table of Nutrient Retention Factors," Release 6, US Department of Agriculture, Agricultural Research Service, Beltsville Human Nutrition Research Center, Maryland, December 2007, http://www.ars.usda.gov/SP2UserFiles/Place/80400525/Data/retn/retn06.pdf.

8. "About the Food and Drug Administration," US Food and Drug Administration, June 18, 2009, http://www.fda.gov/AboutFDA/WhatWeDo/WhatFDADoesn'tRegulate/default.htm.

9. Judith E. Foulke, "A Fresh Look at Food Preservatives," *FDA Consumer*, US Food and Drug Administration, October 1993, http://www.cfsan.fda.gov/~dms/fdpreser.html.

10. "Food Ingredients Backgrounder," 2007–2009 IFIC Foundation Media Guide on Food Safety and Nutrition, accessed October 10, 2008, http://ific.org.

11. Lynne Olver, "Food Timeline FAQs: MesopotamiaThrough Shakespeare," *Food Timeline*, July 12, 2009, http://www.foodtimeline.org/foodfaq3.html#egypt.

12. Marshall Brain, "How Food Preservation Works," *How Stuff Works*, October 30, 2008, http://recipes.howstuffworks.com/food-preservation.htm.

13. Ibid., 2.

14. Charlotte P. Brennand, "Ten Most Commonly Asked Questions About Food Irradiation Food Fact Safety Sheet" March 1995, FN-250.8, Idaho State University Radiation Information Network's Food Irradiation, http://www.physics.isu.edu/radinf/food.htm.

15. Brain, 2.

Chapter 3: Churning Out Food

1. Daniel R. Ess, "Ag101: Demographics," US Environmental Protection Agency, Purdue Research Foundation. April 14, 2013, http://www.epa.gov/oecaagct/ag101/demographics.html.

2. Jim Goodman, "We Need to Eat Locally Again," *The Cornucopia Institute*, August 4, 2008, www.cornucopia.org/2008/08/we-need-to-eat-locally-again.

3. James E. Horne and Maura McDermott, *The Next Green Revolution: Essential Steps to a Healthy, Sustainable Agriculture* (New York: Good Products Press/Hawthorn Press, 2001), 10.

4. Jane Frankenberger, "Ag101: Crop Production," US Environmental Protection Agency, Purdue Research Foundation, August 10, 2012, http://www.epa.gov/oecaagct/ag101/crop.html.

5. "Label Lowdown: Cruelty Free," Whole Living, *Body + Soul* magazine, September 2008, 28.

6. "Taking a Bite Out of Climate Change," *Sustainable Table*, Food Program, Grace Communications Foundations, accessed June 29, 2015, http://www.sustainabletable.org/982/agriculture-energy-climate-change.

7. "Ethylene Facts" *Catalytic Generators*, accessed June 30, 2015, http://www.catalyticgenerators.com/whatisethylene.html.

8. Don G. Jones, "Ag101: Pork Production," US Environmental Protection Agency, Purdue Research Foundation, April 12, 2013, http://www.epa.gov/oecaagct/ag101/pork.html.

9. David Harvey, "Poultry and Eggs: Background," USDA Economic Research Service, May 28, 2012, http://www.ers.usda.gov/topics/animal-products/poultry-eggs/background.aspx.

10. Kenneth Matthews, "Livestock, Dairy, and Poultry Outlook," Economic Research Service, US Department of Agriculture, July 17, 2013, http://www.ers.usda.gov/media/1174716/ldpm229.pdf.

11. Tom Applegate, "Ag101: Poultry Production," US Environmental Protection Agency, Purdue Research Foundation, June 27, 2012, www.epa/gov/oecaagct/ag101/poultry.html.

12. Horne, 43.

13. Ibid., 42–56

14. Bryan A. McCarty, "Local vs Organic Conundrum," *Keep Green Going*, Environmental News Network, March 21, 2008, http://www.enn.com.

15. Lisa Roberts, "The Good and Bad About Organics," *Orlando Sentinel*, Environmental News Network, February 22, 2006, http://www.enn.com.

16. Libby Quaid, "Parents Worried About Pesticides Turn to Organic Food," *Associated Press*, November 3, 2005, Environmental News Network, http://www.enn.com.

17. Roberts.

18. Christie Matheson, "The World's Best Diet," *Body + Soul* magazine, June 2008, 98.

19. Michael Pollan, "Back to the Heart of Organics," *Utne*, September–October 2004, 92.

20. Ibid.

21. Ibid.

22. Ibid.

23. Ibid.

Chapter 4: Feeding the Masses

1. James E. Horne and Maura McDermott, *The Next Green Revolution: Essential Steps to a Healthy, Sustainable Agriculture* (New York: Good Products Press/Hawthorn Press, 2001), 15–16.

2. Leon Hesser, *The Man Who Fed the World: An Authorized Biography of Nobel Peace Prize Laureate Norman Borlaug and His Battle to End World Hunger* (Dallas, Tex.: Durban House, 2006), 61.

3. Ibid., 42.

4. Ibid., 41.

5. Ibid., 54.

6. Ibid., 41.

7. Ibid., 57.

8. "Helping Hungry Families Feed Themselves," *Heifer International*, accessed November 12, 2008, http://www.heifer.org.

9. Terry L. Anderson and Bruce Yandle, eds., *Agriculture and the Environment: Searching for Greener Pastures* (Stanford, Calif.: Stanford University/Hoover Institution Press, 2001).

10. Horne, 16.

11. "FDA Releases Final Guidance on Genetically Engineered Animals," US Food and Drug Administration, January 15, 2009, http://www.fda/gov/ForConsumers/ConsumerUpdates/ucm092738.htm.

12. "Genetically Modified Foods," *Healthline*, accessed February 22, 2009, http://www.healthline.com/adamcontent/genetically-engineered-foods.htm.

13. Jim Goodman, "We Need to Eat Locally Again," *The Cornucopia Institute*, August 4, 2008, www.cornucopia.org/2008/08/we-need-to-eat-locally-again.

14. "Legacy of Rachel Carson's Silent Spring," *American Chemical Society*, June 30, 2015, http://www.acs.org/content/acs/en/education/whatischemistry/landmarks/Rachel-carson-silent-spring.html.

15. Goodman, 2.

16. "Environmental and Development Changes: The Imperative to Act," The Blue Planet Prize laureates, February 20, 2012, The Asahi Glass Foundation, 14, http://www.af-info.or.jp/en/bpplaureates/index.html.

Chapter 5: Harvests at Risk

1. Eric Holt Gimenez, "We Already Grow Enough Food For 10 Billion People—and Still Can't End Hunger," May 2, 2012, updated December 18, 2014, Huffpost Taste, *Huffington Post.*, http://huffingtonpost.com/eric-holt-gimenez/world-hunger_b_1463429.html.

2. Elizabeth Royte, "One-Third of Food Is Lost or Wasted: What Can Be Done," Future of Food, *National Geographic*, October 13, 2014, http://news.nationalgeographic.com/news/2014/10/141013-food-waste-national-security-environment-science-ngfood/.

3. Daniel R. Ess, "Ag101: Demographics," US Environmental Protection Agency, Purdue Research Foundation, April 14, 2013, http://www.epa.gov/oecaagct/ag101/demographics.html.

4. "Environmental and Development Changes: The Imperative to Act," The Blue Planet Prize laureates, February 20, 2012, The Asahi Glass Foundation, 9, 21–22, http://www.af-info.or.jp/en/bpplaureates/index.html.

5. Ibid, 13–14.

6. James E. Horne and Maura McDermott, *The Next Green Revolution: Essential Steps to a Healthy, Sustainable Agriculture* (New York: Good Products Press/Hawthorn Press, 2001).

7. Ibid.

8. Ibid, 10.

9. Ibid.

10. Ana Sofia Joanes, *Fresh*, Ripple Effect Productions (New York: New Video Group, 2012).

11. Horne, 11.

12. Ibid, 10.

13. Jim Goodman, "We Need to Eat Locally Again," *The Cornucopia Institute*, August 4, 2008, www.cornucopia.org/2008/08/we-need-to-eat-locally-again.

14. Blue Planet Prize report

15. Horne, p. 11.

16. David Mackay, "How Drought Is Parching the World's Food Industry," *Foodprocessing Technology*, September 29, 2008, http://www.foodprocessing-technology.com/features/feature42194/.

17. Ibid.

18. Ibid., 2.

19. Robert Bates, *Ingredients*, Center for Independent Documentary (New York: New Video Group, 2011).

20. John Riddell, "Naomi Klein: 'Only Mass Social Movements Can Save Us'," Book Review, *Climate and Capitalism*, October 19, 2014, http://climateand capitalism.com/2014/10/19/Naomi-klein-climate-change-mass-social-movements-can-save-us/.

21. "Overview of Greenhouse Gases," Climate Change, Environmental Protection Agency, accessed June 30, 2015, http://epa.gov/climatechange/ghgemissions/gases/ch4.html.

22. "Climate Impacts on Agriculture and Food Supply," Climate Change, Environmental Protection Agency, September 9, 2013, http://www.epa.gov/climatechange/impacts-adaption/agriculture.html.

23. Elizabeth Royte, "One-Third of Food Is Lost or Wasted: What Can Be Done," Future of Food, *National Geographic*, October 12, 2014, http://news.nationalgeographic.com/news/2014/10/141013-food-waste-national-security-environment-science-ngfood/.

24. Horne, 16.

25. Ibid.

26. Ibid., 17.

27. Ibid., 16.

28. Ibid., 17.

29. Lindsay Gulla, "Should Teens Have Protein?" *Livestrong.com*, February 23, 2014, http://www.livestrong.com/article/431401-should-teens-have-protein/.

30. Pollan, 92.

Chapter 6: Ever-Green Agroecology

1. Naomi Klein, *This Changes Everything: Capitalism vs. the Climate* (New York: Simon & Schuster), 2104, 134.

2. Ian Fitzpatrick, "Can We Start Talking About Food and Agriculture in the Runup to Paris?" *The Leap*, March 6, 2015, http://theleap.thischangeseverything.org/can-we-start-talking-about-food-and-agriculture-in-the-runup-to-paris/.

3. "Exploring Sustainability in Agriculture," Opportunities in Agriculture Bulletin, *Sustainable Agriculture and Research Education*, accessed September 27, 2008, http://www.sare.org/publications/explore/index.htm.

4. James E. Horne and Maura McDermott, *The Next Green Revolution: Essential Steps to a Healthy, Sustainable Agriculture* (New York: Good Products Press/Hawthorn Press, 2001), 37.

5. Ibid., 35.

6. "Exploring Sustainability in Agriculture," Opportunities in Agriculture Bulletin, *Sustainable Agriculture and Research Education*, accessed September 27, 2008, http://www.sare.org/publications/explore/index.htm.

7. Horne, 55.

8. Fitzpatrick.

9. Ibid.

10. Klein, 135–136

11. M.S. Swaminathan, "Rio +20: Green Economy with Inclusive Growth," Blue Planet Prize report, 113.

12. Elizabeth Weise, "Soil Program Reaps World Food Prize," *USA Today*, October 24, 2002, 10d.

13. Ibid.

14. Ibid.

15. Ibid.

16. "Farm to Save Energy, Curb Pollution," Learning Center Bulletins, Sustainable Agriculture Research and Education, 2012, http://www.sare.org/Learning-Center/Bulletins/Clean-Energy-Farming/Text-Version/Farm-to-Save-Energy.

17. Sustainable Table, "Fossil Fuel and Energy Use," Serving Up Healthy Food Choices whitepaper, 1, accessed July 22, 2015, http://www.nyu.edu/sustainability/pdf/Fossil%20Fuel%20and%20Energy%20Use%202%20FCSummit-HO-20091207.pdf.

18. "Clean Energy Farming," Opportunities in Agriculture Bulletin, Sustainable Agriculture Research and Education, accessed July 22, 2015, http://www.sare.org/Learning-Center/Bulletins/Clean-Energy-Farming/.

19. Christie Matheson, "The World's Best Diet," *Body + Soul* magazine, June 2008, 97.

20. "Take a Bite Out of Climate Change," Agriculture, Energy & Climate Change, Sustainable Table Web site, accessed June 30, 2015, http://www.sustainabletable.org/982/agriculture-energy-climate-change.

21. Rebecca Nelson, "Opportunities and Solutions for Sustainable Food Production," *Sustainable Development Solutions Network*, January 15, 2013, 8, http://unsdsn.org/wp-content/uploads/2014/02/130112-HLP-TG7-Solutions-for-sustainable-food-production.pdf.

22. Anastasia Masurat, "The Future of Farming: Outsmarting GM." *The Utne Reader*, September/October, 2004, 100.

23. Ibid.

24. Ibid.

25. Ibid.

Chapter 7: Fixing the Food Chain

1. Julie Bizzozero, "U.S. Teens Spend $16 Billion on Food Annually," Trending Food, May 14, 2014, foodproductdesign.com/blogs/trending-foods/2014/05/u-s-teens-spend-16-billion-on-food.aspx.

2. "Take a Bite Out of Climate Change," Agriculture, Energy & Climate Change, *Sustainable Table*, accessed June 30, 2015, http://www.sustainabletable.org/982/agriculture-energy-climate-change.

3. Jim Goodman, "Farmer Markets: Think Local as Well as Organic," *Organic Consumers Association*, Environmental News Network, July 25, 2008, http://www.enn.com.

4. Lori Silverbush, *A Place at the Table: the Crisis of 49 Million Hungry Americans and How to Solve It* (Los Angeles: Magnolia Pictures, 2013).

5. "Green + Teen = Enriching Summer," Longacre Farm press release, January 14, 2008.

6. Lori Wright, "University of New Hampshire Launches Groundbreaking EcoGastronomy Program: First-of-its-kind program educates students about sustainable food systems," from Industry News at *Hospitality Net*, September 2, 2008, http://www.hospitalitynet.org.

7. Heather Clark, "Urban Farms Grow as Cities Seek Safe, Cheap Food," *Ag News*, September 2, 2008, http://www.agweekly.com.

8. "Urban Nonprofit Launches a Food-Access Revolution," What is Sustainable Agriculture?, Best Practice Sampler, SARE, 7, http://www.sare.org/Learning-Center/SARE-Program-Materials/National-Program-Materials/What-is-Sustainable-Agriculture.

9. Clark.

10. "Community Supported Agriculture," *Alternative Farming Systems Information Center*, December 12, 2014, http://www.nal.usda.gov/afsic/pubs/csa/csa.shtml.

11. Michael Pollan, "Back to the Heart of Organics," *Utne*, September–October 2004, 94.

12. Ibid.

GLOSSARY

artificial—Not from nature; man-made or created in a laboratory.

conventional—The usual way to do something; following a traditional pattern.

crossbreeding—Interbreeding or blending elements of two different plants or animals.

DNA—Deoxyribonucleic acid; a substance present in the center of almost every cell in every living thing that contains genetic information.

ethylene—A hormone that speeds up the sequences of growth, development, ripening, and aging in plants; also, a byproduct of propane-, diesel-, and gasoline-powered engines.

factory farm—A large farm owned by a company and run like a factory to limit costs and increase profit.

fertilizer—Either a chemical or natural material, such as manure, added to soil to increase growth of plants.

genetic modification (GM)—Changing a plant or animal's structure by removing DNA and replacing it with that of another plant or animal.

high-yield crops—Crops bred for larger than normal harvest.

hybrid—The offspring of two different varieties of plants or animals; something made by combining different elements.

industrial farming—Large farms that use large equipment to produce more food.

macronutrients—Nutrients needed by the body in large amounts, such as proteins and carbohydrates.

methane—A chemical element; second most common greenhouse gas.

micronutrients—Nutrients needed by the body in small amounts, such as vitamins and minerals.

microorganism—A microscopic living thing, such as a virus, fungus, or bacterium.

monoculture—Crops of a single type of plant; growing the same crop in the same plot of land year after year.

natural—Coming from nature; not made, treated, or changed by humans.

nitrogen—A chemical element that makes up about 78 percent of the earth's atmosphere.

nutrition—The nourishment that the body uses for growth and life.

organic—Coming from living matter; not grown or produced with chemicals or man-made fertilizers.

pesticide—A substance used to kill insects and other pests.

phosphorus—A natural mineral used to fertilize crops.

polyculture farming—Many different crops grown on an expanse of land; growing different crops side-by-side or rotating crop fields.

processing—A series of steps to change food for packing or to treat food to preserve it.

production—The action of making or processing something.

residue—The part of a plant left after harvest; the roots and stem or stalk on top of the soil. A film or small amount of something left after washing.

shuttle-breeding—Sending seeds back and forth between two plots of land for planting so new seeds can be used in crossbreeding. This speeds up the development of new plant varieties.

sustainable—Able to be kept up or maintained.

synthetic—Artificial; man-made.

FURTHER READING

Fleischman, Paul. *Eyes Wide Open: Going Behind the Environmental Headlines.* Somerville, MA: Candlewick Press, 2014.

Francis, Amy, ed. *Organic Food*. Farmington Hills, MI: Greenhaven Press, 2015.

Gay, Kathlyn. *Food: The New Gold*. Minneapolis: Twenty-first Century Books, 2013.

Owings, Lisa. *Sustainable Agriculture.* Minneapolis: ABDO Publishing, 2013.

Singer, Jane E., and Kim Ettingoff. *Wheat: Feeding the World*. Broomall, PA: Mason Crest, 2014.

WEBSITES

Food and Water Watch

foodandwaterwatch.org

Champion healthy food and clean water for all with ideas for taking action to support the environment.

Farm Sanctuary

farmsanctuary.org

Guide to healthy living and mindful eating. Works to prevent cruelty to farm animals and change society's view toward animals and food.

Sustainable Table

sustainabletable.org

Focuses on food, water, and energy and celebrates local sustainable food; educates consumers about sustainable agriculture.

VIDEO AND STREAMING RESOURCES

Bates, Robert. *Ingredients.* Center for Independent Documentary. New York: New Video Group, 2011.

Describes the food crisis in America with obesity and diabetes on the rise, skyrocketing food costs, decline of family farms, and agricultural environment in jeopardy. Explores a thriving local food movement as our world becomes a more flavorless, disconnected, and dangerous place to eat.

Jaud, Jean-Paul, and Gabriel Yared. *Food Beware: The French Organic Revolution.* First-Run Features, 2009.

The mayor of a small French town has changed the school's lunch menu to locally grown organic foods to bring safe food products and a healthy diet to the children. We learn about the abuses of the food industry, the challenges and rewards of safe food production, and practical solutions we can all take part in.

Joanes, Ana Sofia. *Fresh.* Ripple Effect Productions. New York: New Video Group, 2012.

Celebrates the farmers, thinkers, and businesspeople across America who are reinventing our food system. Offers a practical vision for the future of our food and our planet.

Silverbush, Lori. *A Place at the Table: the Crisis of 49 Million Hungry Americans and How to Solve it.* Los Angeles: Magnolia Pictures, 2013.

Examines hunger in America and proposes ways to solve it.

INDEX